ENGLISH DIALECTS

From the Eighth Century to the Present Day

Rev. Walter W. Skeat,
LITT.D., D.C.L., LL.D., PH.D., F.B.A. Elrington and Bosworth Professor of Anglo-Saxon and Fellow of Christ's College. Founder and formerly Director of the English Dialect Society

"English in the native garb;"
K. Henry V. v. i. 80

Eikon Publications

Eikon Publications

First published by Cambridge University Press in 1911.
This facsimile edition published by Eikon in 2011.

ISBN: 978-1-4477-8051-9

PREFACE

THE following brief sketch is an attempt to present, in a popular form, the history of our English dialects, from the eighth century to the present day. The evidence, which is necessarily somewhat imperfect, goes to show that the older dialects appear to have been few in number, each being tolerably uniform over a wide area; and that the rather numerous dialects of the present day were gradually developed by the breaking up of the older groups into subdialects. This is especially true of the old Northumbrian dialect, in which the speech of Aberdeen was hardly distinguishable from that of Yorkshire, down to the end of the fourteenth century; soon after which date, the use of it for literary purposes survived in Scotland only. The chief literary dialect, in the earliest period, was Northumbrian or "Anglian," down to the middle of the ninth century. After that time our literature was mostly in the Southern or Wessex dialect, commonly called "Anglo-Saxon," the dominion of which lasted down to the early years of the thirteenth century, when the East Midland dialect surely but gradually rose to pre-eminence, and has now become the speech of the empire. Towards this result the two great universities contributed not a little. I proceed to discuss the foreign elements found in our dialects, the chief being Scandinavian and French. The influence of the former has long been acknowledged; a due recognition of the importance of the latter has yet to come. In conclusion, I give some selected specimens of the use of the modern dialects.

I beg leave to thank my friend Mr P. Giles, M.A., Hon. LL.D. of Aberdeen, and University Reader in Comparative Philology, for a few hints and for kindly advice.

W. W. S.

CAMBRIDGE
3 *March* 1911

TABLE OF CONTENTS

*** *For a transcription of the Facsimile see* pp. 75–6.

CHAPTER I

DIALECTS AND THEIR VALUE

ACCORDING to the New English Dictionary, the oldest sense, in English, of the word *dialect* was simply "a manner of speaking" or "phraseology," in accordance with its derivation from the Greek *dialectos*, a discourse or way of speaking; from the verb *dialegesthai*, to discourse or converse.

The modern meaning is somewhat more precise. In relation to a language such as English, it is used in a special sense to signify "a local variety of speech differing from the standard or literary language." When we talk of "speakers of dialect," we imply that they employ a provincial method of speech to which the man who has been educated to use the language of books is unaccustomed. Such a man finds that the dialect-speaker frequently uses words or modes of expression which he does not understand or which are at any rate strange to him; and he is sure to notice that such words as seem to be familiar to him are, for the most part, strangely pronounced. Such differences are especially noticeable in the use of vowels and diphthongs, and in the mode of intonation.

The speaker of the "standard" language is frequently tempted to consider himself as the dialect-speaker's superior, unless he has already acquired some elementary knowledge of the value of the science of language or has sufficient common sense to be desirous of learning to understand that which for the moment lies beyond him. I remember once hearing the remark made—"What is the good of dialects? Why not sweep them all away, and have done with them?" But the very form of the question betrays ignorance of the facts; for it is no more possible to do away with them than it is possible to suppress the waves of the sea. English, like every other literary language, has always had its dialects and will long continue to possess them in secluded districts, though they are at the present time losing much of that archaic character which gives them their chief value. The spread of education may profoundly modify them, but the spoken language of the people will ever continue to devise new variations and to initiate developments of its own. Even the "standard" language is continually losing old words and admitting new ones, as was noted long ago by Horace; and our so-called "standard" pronunciation is ever imperceptibly but surely changing, and never continues in one stay.

In the very valuable *Lectures on the Science of Language* by Professor F. Max Müller, the second Lecture, which deserves careful study, is chiefly occupied by some account of the processes which he names respectively "phonetic decay" and "dialectic regeneration"; processes to which all languages have always been and ever will be subject.

By "phonetic decay" is meant that insidious and gradual alteration in the sounds of spoken words which, though it cannot be prevented, at last so corrupts a word that it becomes almost or wholly unmeaning. Such a word as *twenty* does not suggest its origin. Many might perhaps guess, from their observation of such numbers as *thirty*, *forty*, etc., that the suffix *-ty* may have something to do with *ten*, of the original of which it is in fact an extremely reduced form; but it is less obvious that *twen-* is a shortened form of *twain*. And perhaps none but scholars of Teutonic languages are aware that *twain* was once of the masculine gender only, while *two* was so restricted that it could only be applied to things that were feminine or neuter. As a somewhat hackneyed example of phonetic decay, we may take the case of the Latin *mea domina*, i.e. my mistress, which became in French *ma dame*, and in English *madam*; and the last of these has been further shortened to *mam*, and even to *'m*, as in the phrase "Yes, 'm." This shows how nine letters may be reduced to one. Similarly, our monosyllable *alms* is all that is left of the Greek *eleēmosynē.* Ten letters have here been reduced to four.

This irresistible tendency to indistinctness and loss is not, however, wholly bad; for it has at the same time largely contributed, especially in English, to such a simplification of grammatical inflexions as certainly has the practical convenience of giving us less to learn. But in addition to this decay in the forms of words, we have also to reckon with a depreciation or weakening of the ideas they express. Many words become so hackneyed as to be no longer impressive. As late as in 1820, Keats could say, in stanza 6 of his poem of *Isabella,* that "His heart beat awfully against his side"; but at the present day the word *awfully* is suggestive of schoolboys' slang. It is here that we may well have the benefit of the principle of "dialectic regeneration." We shall often do well to borrow from our dialects many terms that are still fresh and racy, and instinct with a full significance. Tennyson was well aware of this, and not only wrote several poems wholly in the Lincolnshire dialect, but introduced dialect words elsewhere. Thus in *The Voyage of Maeldune,* he has the striking line: "Our voices were thinner and fainter than any flittermouse-shriek." In at least sixteen dialects a *flittermouse* means "a bat."

I have mentioned Tennyson in this connexion

because he was a careful student of English, not only in its dialectal but also in its older forms. But, as a matter of fact, nearly all our chief writers have recognised the value of dialectal words. Tennyson was not the first to use the above word. Near the end of the Second Act of his *Sad Shepherd*, Ben Jonson speaks of:

> Green-bellied snakes, blue fire-drakes in the sky,
> And giddy flitter-mice with leather wings.

Similarly, there are plenty of "provincialisms" in Shakespeare. In an interesting book entitled *Shakespeare, his Birthplace and its Neighbourhood*, by J. R. Wise, there is a chapter on "The Provincialisms of Shakespeare," from which I beg leave to give a short extract by way of specimen. "There is the expressive compound 'blood-boltered' in *Macbeth* (Act IV, Sc. 1), which the critics have all thought meant simply blood-stained. Miss Baker, in her *Glossary of Northamptonshire Words*, first pointed out that 'bolter' was peculiarly a Warwickshire word, signifying to clot, collect, or cake, as snow does in a horse's hoof, thus giving the phrase a far greater intensity of meaning. And Steevens, too, first noticed that in the expression in *The Winter's Tale* (Act III, Sc. 3), 'Is it a boy or a child?'—where, by the way, every actor tries to make a point, and the audience invariably laughs—the word 'child' is used, as is sometimes the case in the midland districts, as synonymous with girl; which is plainly its meaning in this passage, although the speaker has used it just before in its more common sense of either a boy or a girl." In fact, the *English Dialect Dictionary* cites the phrase "is it a lad or a child?" as being still current in Shropshire; and duly states that, in Warwickshire, "dirt collected on the hairs of a horse's leg and forming into hard masses is said to *bolter*." Trench further points out that many of our pure Anglo-Saxon words which lived on into the formation of our early English, subsequently dropped out of our usual vocabulary, and are now to be found only in the dialects. A good example is the word *eme*, an uncle (A.S. *ēam*), which is rather common in Middle English, but has seldom appeared in our literature since the time of Drayton. Yet it is well known in our Northern dialects, and Sir Walter Scott puts the expression "Didna his *eme* die" in the mouth of Davie Deans (*Heart of Midlothian*, ch. XII). In fact, few things are more extraordinary in the history of our language than the singularly capricious manner in which good and useful words emerge into or disappear from use in "standard" talk, for no very obvious reason. Such a word as *yonder* is common enough still; but its corresponding adjective *yon*, as in the phrase "yon man," is usually relegated to our dialects. Though it is common in Shakespeare, it is comparatively rare in the Middle English period, from the twelfth to the fifteenth century. It only occurs once in Chaucer, where it is introduced as being a Northern word; and it absolutely disappears from record in the tenth, eleventh, and twelfth centuries. Bosworth's *Anglo-Saxon Dictionary* gives no example of its use, and it was long supposed that it would be impossible to trace it in our early records. Nevertheless, when Dr Sweet printed, for the first time, an edition of King Alfred's translation of Pope Gregory's *Pastoral Care*, an example appeared in which it was employed in the most natural manner, as if it were in everyday use. At p. 443 of that treatise is the sentence—"Aris and gong to geonre byrg," i.e. Arise and go to yon city. Here the A.S. *geon* (pronounced like the modern *yon*) is actually declined after the regular manner, being duly provided with the suffix *-re*, which was the special suffix reserved only for the genitive or dative feminine. It is here a dative after the preposition *to*.

There is, in fact, no limit to the good use to which a reverent study of our dialects may be put by a diligent student. They abound with pearls which are worthy of a better fate than to be trampled under foot. I will content myself with giving one last example that is really too curious to be passed over in silence.

It so happens that in the Anglo-Saxon epic poem of *Beowulf*, one of the most remarkable and precious of our early poems, there is a splendid and graphic description of a lonely mere, such as would have delighted the heart of Edgar Allan Poe, the author of *Ulalume.* In Professor Earle's prose translation of this passage, given in his *Deeds of Beowulf*, at p. 44, is a description of two mysterious monsters, of whom it is said that "they inhabit unvisited land, wolf-crags, windy bluffs, the dread fen-track, where the mountain waterfall amid precipitous gloom vanisheth beneath—flood under earth. Not far hence it is, reckoning by miles, that the Mere standeth, and over it hang rimy groves; a wood with clenched roots overshrouds the water." The word to be noted here is the word *rimy*, i.e. covered with rime or hoar-frost. The original Anglo-Saxon text has the form *hrinde*, the meaning of which was long doubtful. Grein, the great German scholar, writing in 1864, acknowledged that he did not know what was intended, and it was not till 1880 that light was first thrown upon the passage. In that year Dr Morris edited, for the first time, some Anglo-Saxon homilies (commonly known as the *Blickling Homilies*, because the MS. is in the library of Blickling Hall, Norfolk); and he called attention to a passage (at p. 209) where the homilist was obviously referring to the lonely mere of the old poem, in which its overhanging groves were described as being *hrimige*, which is nothing but the true old spelling of *rimy*. He naturally concluded that the word *hrinde* (in the MS. of Beowulf) was miswritten, and that the scribe had inadvertently put down *hrinde* instead of *hrimge*, which is a legitimate contraction of *hrimige*. Many scholars accepted this solution; but a further light was yet to come, viz. in 1904. In that year, Dr Joseph Wright printed the fifth volume of the *English Dialect Dictionary*, showing that in the dialects of Scotland, Northumberland, Durham, and Yorkshire, the word for "hoarfrost" is not *rime*, but *rind*, with a derived adjective *rindy*, which has the same sense as *rimy*. At the same time, he called attention yet once more to the passage in *Beowulf*. It is established, accordingly, that the suspected mistake in the MS. is no mistake at all; that the form *hrinde* is correct, being a contraction of *hrindge* or *hrindige*, plural of the adjective *hrindig*, which is preserved in our dialects, in the form *rindy*, to this very day. In direct contradiction of a common popular error that regards our dialectal forms as being, for the most part, "corrupt," it will be found by experience that they are remarkably conservative and antique.

CHAPTER II

DIALECTS IN EARLY TIMES

THE history of our dialects in the earliest periods of which we have any record is necessarily somewhat obscure, owing to the scarcity of the documents that have come down to us. The earliest of these have been carefully collected and printed in one volume by Dr Sweet, entitled *The Oldest English Texts*, edited for the Early English Text Society in 1885. Here we already find the existence of no less than four dialects, which have been called by the names of Northumbrian, Mercian, Wessex (or Anglo-Saxon), and Kentish. These correspond, respectively, though not quite exactly, to what we may roughly call Northern, Midland, Southern, and Kentish. Whether the limits of these dialects were always the same from the earliest times, we cannot tell; probably not, when the unsettled state of the country is considered, in the days when repeated invasions of the Danes and Norsemen necessitated constant efforts to repel them. It is therefore sufficient to define the areas covered by these dialects in quite a rough way. We may regard the Northumbrian or Northern as the dialect or group of dialects spoken to the north of the river Humber, as the name implies; the Wessex or Southern, as the dialect or group of dialects spoken to the south of the river Thames; the Kentish as being peculiar to Kent; and the Mercian as in use in the Midland districts, chiefly to the south of the Humber and to the north of the Thames. The modern limits are somewhat different, but the above division of the three chief dialects (excluding Kentish) into Northern, Midland, and Southern is sufficient for taking a broad general view of the language in the days before the Norman Conquest.

The investigation of the differences of dialect in our early documents only dates from 1885, owing to the previous impossibility of obtaining access to these oldest texts. Before that date, it so happened that nearly all the manuscripts that had been printed or examined were in one and the same dialect, viz. the Southern (or Wessex). The language employed in these was (somewhat unhappily) named "Anglo-Saxon"; and the very natural mistake was made of supposing that this "Anglo-Saxon" was the sole language (or dialect) which served for all the "Angles" and "Saxons" to be found in the "land of the Angles" or England. This is the reason why it is desirable to give the more general name of "Old English" to the oldest forms of our language, because this term can be employed collectively, so as to include Northumbrian, Mercian, "Anglo-Saxon" and Kentish under one designation. The name "Anglo-Saxon" was certainly rather inappropriate, as the speakers of it were mostly Saxons and not Angles at all; which leads up to the paradox that they did not speak "English"; for that, in the extreme literal sense, was the language of the Angles only! But now that the true relationship of the old dialects is known, it is not uncommon for scholars to speak of the Wessex dialect as "Saxon," and of the Northumbrian and Mercian dialects as "Anglian"; for the latter are found to have some features in common that differ sharply from those found in "Saxon."

Manuscripts in the Southern dialect are fairly abundant, and contain poems, homilies, land-charters, laws, wills, translations of Latin treatises, glossaries, etc.; so that there is considerable variety. One of the most precious documents is the history known as the *Anglo-Saxon Chronicle*, which was continued even after the Conquest till the year 1154, when the death and burial of King Stephen were duly recorded.

But specimens of the oldest forms of the Northern and Midland dialects are, on the other hand, very much fewer in number than students of our language desire, and are consequently deserving of special mention. They are duly enumerated in the chapters below, which discuss these dialects separately.

Having thus sketched out the broad divisions into which our dialects may be distributed, I shall proceed to enter upon a particular discussion of each group, beginning with the Northern or Northumbrian.

CHAPTER III

THE DIALECTS OF NORTHUMBRIA; TILL A.D. 1000

In Professor Earle's excellent manual on Anglo-Saxon Literature, chapter V is entirely occupied with "the Anglian Period," and begins thus:—"While Canterbury was so important a seminary of learning, there was, in the Anglian region of Northumbria, a development of religious and intellectual life which makes it natural to regard the whole brilliant period from the later seventh to the early ninth century as the Anglian Period....Anglia became for a century the light-spot of European history; and we here recognise the first great stage in the revival of learning, and the first movement towards the establishment of public order in things temporal and spiritual."

Unfortunately for the student of English, though perhaps fortunately for the historian, the most important book belonging to this period was written in Latin. This was the *Historia Ecclesiastica Gentis Anglorum*, or the Church History of the Anglian

People. The writer was Beda, better known as "the Venerable Bede," who was born near Wearmouth (Durham) in 672, and lived for the greater part of his life at Jarrow, where he died in 735. He wrote several other works, also in Latin, most of which Professor Earle enumerates. It is said of Beda himself that he was "learned in our native songs," and it is probable that he wrote many things in his native Northumbrian or Durham dialect; but they have all perished, with the exception of one precious fragment of five lines, printed by Dr Sweet (at p. 149) from the St Gall MS. No. 254, of the ninth century. It is usually called Beda's Death-song, and is here given:

Fore there neidfaerae naenig uuiurthit
thonc-snotturra than him thar[f] sie,
to ymbhycggannae, aer his hin-iong[a]e,
huaet his gastae, godaes aeththa yflaes,
aefter deoth-daege doemid uueorth[a]e.

Literally translated, this runs as follows:

Before the need-journey no one becomes
more wise in thought than he ought to be,
(in order) to contemplate, ere his going hence,
what for his spirit, (either) of good or of evil,
after (his) death-day, will be adjudged.

It is from Beda's *Church History*, Book IV, chap. 24 (or 22), that we learn the story of Cædmon, the famous Northumbrian poet, who was a herdsman and lay brother in the abbey of Whitby, in the days of the abbess Hild, who died in 680, near the close of the seventh century. He received the gift of divine song in a vision of the night; and after the recognition by the abbess and others of his heavenly call, became a member of the religious fraternity, and devoted the rest of his life to the composition of sacred poetry.

He sang (says Beda) the Creation of the world, the origin of the human race, and all the history of Genesis; the departure of Israel out of Egypt and their entrance into the land of promise, with many other histories from holy writ; the incarnation, passion, and resurrection of our Lord, and His ascension into heaven; the coming of the Holy Spirit and the teaching of the Apostles. Likewise of the terror of the future judgement, the horror of punishment in hell, and the bliss of the heavenly kingdom he made many poems; and moreover, many others concerning divine benefits and judgements; in all which he sought to wean men from the love of sin, and to stimulate them to the enjoyment and pursuit of good action.

It happens that we still possess some poems which answer more or less to this description; but they are all of later date and are only known from copies written in the Southern dialect of Wessex; and, as the original Northumbrian text has unfortunately perished, we have no means of knowing to what extent they represent Cædmon's work. It is possible that they preserve some of it in a more or less close form of translation, but we cannot verify this possibility. It has been ascertained, on the other hand, that a certain portion (but by no means all) of these poems is adapted, with but slight change, from an original poem written in the Old Saxon of the continent.

Nevertheless, it so happens that a short hymn of nine lines has been preserved nearly in the original form, as Cædmon dictated it; and it corresponds closely with Beda's Latin version. It is found at the end of the Cambridge MS. of Beda's *Historia Ecclesiastica* in the following form:

Nu scylun hergan hefaenricaes uard,
metudæs maecti end his modgidanc,
uerc uuldurfadur; sue he uundra gihuaes,
eci Dryctin, or astelidæ.
He aerist scop aelda barnum
heben til hrofe, haleg scepen[d].
Tha middungeard moncynnæs uard,
eci Dryctin, æfter tiadæ
firum fold[u], frea allmectig.

I here subjoin a literal translation.

Now ought we to praise the warden of heaven's realm,
the Creator's might and His mind's thought,
the works of the Father of glory; (even) as He, of every wonder,
(being) eternal Ruler, established the beginning.
He first (of all) shaped, for the sons of men,
heaven as (their) roof, (He) the holy Creator.
The middle world (He), mankind's warden,
eternal Ruler, afterwards prepared,
the world for men—(being the) Almighty Lord.

The locality of these lines is easily settled, as we

may assign them to Whitby. Similarly, Beda's Death-song may be assigned to the county of Durham.

A third poem, extending to fourteen lines, may be called the "Northumbrian Riddle." It is called by Dr Sweet the "Leiden Riddle," because the MS. that contains it is now at Leyden, in Holland. The locality is unknown, but we may assign it to Yorkshire or Durham without going far wrong. There is another copy in a Southern dialect. These three brief poems, viz. Beda's Death-song, Cædmon's Hymn, and the Riddle, are all printed, accessibly, in Sweet's *Anglo-Saxon Reader.*

There is another relic of Old Northumbrian, apparently belonging to the middle of the eighth century, which is too remarkable to be passed over. I refer to the famous Ruthwell cross, situate not far to the west of Annan, near the southern coast of Dumfriesshire, and near the English border. On each of its four faces it bears inscriptions; on two opposite faces in Latin, and on the other two in runic characters. Each of the latter pair contains a few lines of Northern poetry, selected from a poem (doubtless by the poet Cynewulf) which is preserved in full in a much later Southern (or Wessex) copy in a MS. at Vercelli in Piedmont (Italy). On the side which Professor Stephens calls the *front* of the cross, the runic inscriptions give us two quotations, both imperfect at the end; and the same is true of the opposite side or *back*. The MS. helps us to restore letters that are missing or broken, and in this way we can be tolerably sure of the correct readings.

The two quotations in front are as follows: it will be seen that the cross itself is supposed to be the speaker.

1. [on]geredæ hinæ god almechttig
tha he walde on galgu gistiga,
modig fore allæ men; buga [ic ni darstæ.]
2. [ahof] ic riicnæ kyningc,
heafunæs hlafard; hælda ic ni darstæ.
bismæradu ungket men ba æt-gadre.
ic wæs mith blodæ bistemid bigoten of [his sidan.]

The two quotations at the back are these:

3. Crist wæs on rodi;
hwethræ ther fusæ fearran cwomu
æththilæ til anum; ic thæt al biheald.
sare ic wæs mith sorgum gidrœfid;
hnag [ic hwethræ tham secgum til handa.]
4. mith strelum giwundad
alegdun hiæ hinæ limwœrignæ;
gistoddum him æt his licæs heafdum,
bihealdun hiæ ther heafun[æs hlafard.]

The literal meaning of the lines is as follows:

1. God almighty stripped Himself
when He would mount upon the gallows (the cross),
courageous before all men; I (the cross) durst not bow down.
2. I (the cross) reared up the royal King,
the Lord of heaven; I durst not bend down.
men reviled us two (the cross and Christ) both together.
I was moistened with the blood poured forth from His side.

3. Christ was upon the cross;
howbeit, thither came eagerly from afar
princes to (see) that One; I beheld all that.
sorely was I afflicted with sorrows;
I submitted however to the men's hands.
4. wounded with arrows,
they laid Him down, weary in His limbs.
they stood beside Him, at the head of His corpse.
they beheld there the Lord of heaven.

In the late MS. it is the cross that is wounded by arrows; whereas in the runic inscription it seems to be implied that it was Christ Himself that was so wounded. The allusion is in any case very obscure; but the latter notion makes the better sense, and is capable of being explained by the Norse legend of Balder, who was frequently shot at by the other gods in sport, as he was supposed to be invulnerable; but he was slain thus one day by a shaft made of mistletoe, which alone had power to harm him.

There is also extant a considerable number of very brief inscriptions, such as that on a column at Bewcastle, in Cumberland; but they contribute little to our knowledge except the forms of proper names. The *Liber Vitæ* of Durham, written in the ninth century, contains between three and four thousand such names, but nothing else.

Coming down to the tenth century, we meet with three valuable documents, all of which are connected with Durham, generally known as the Durham Ritual and the Northumbrian Gospels.

The Durham Ritual was edited for the Surtees Society in 1840 by the Rev. J. Stevenson. The MS. is in the Cathedral library at Durham, and contains three distinct Latin service-books, with Northumbrian glosses in various later hands, besides a number of unglossed Latin additions. A small portion of the MS. has been misplaced by the binder; the Latin prose on pp. 138—145 should follow that on p. 162. Mr Stevenson's edition exhibits a rather large number of misreadings, most of which (I fear not quite all) are noted in my "Collation of the Durham Ritual" printed in the *Philological Society's Transactions*, 1877–9, Appendix II. I give, by way of specimen, a curious passage (at p. 192), which tells us all about the eight pounds of material that went to make up the body of Adam.

aehto pundo of thæm aworden is Adam pund lames of thon
Octo pondera de quibus factus est Adam. Pondus limi, inde
aworden is flæsc pund fyres of thon read is blod and hat
factus est caro; pondus ignis, inde rubeus est sanguis et calidus;
pund saltes of thon sindon salto tehero pund deawes of thon
pondus salis, inde sunt salsae lacrimae; pondus roris, unde
aworden is swat pund blostmes of thon is fagung egena
factus est sudor; pondus floris, inde est uarietas oculorum;
pund wolcnes of thon is unstydfullnisse *vel* unstatholfæstnisse thohta
pondus nubis, inde est instabilitas mentium;
pund windes of thon is oroth cald pund gefe of thon is
pondus uenti, inde est anhela frigida: pondus gratiae, id est
thoht monnes
sensus hominis.

We thus learn that Adam's flesh was made of a pound of loam; his red and hot blood, of fire; his salt tears, of salt; his sweat, of dew; the colour of his eyes, of flowers; the instability of his thoughts, of cloud; his cold breath, of wind; and his intelligence, of grace.

The Northumbrian glosses on the four Gospels are contained in two MSS., both of remarkable interest and value. The former of these, sometimes known as the Lindisfarne MS., and sometimes as the Durham Book, is now MS. Cotton, Nero D. 4 in the British Museum, and is one of the chief treasures in our national collection. It contains a beautifully executed Latin text of the four Gospels, written in the isle of Lindisfarne, by Eadfrith (bishop of Lindisfarne in 698—721), probably before 700. The interlinear Northumbrian gloss is two and a half centuries later, and was made by Aldred, a priest, about 950, at a time when the MS. was kept at Chester-le-Street, near Durham, whither it had been removed for greater safety. Somewhat later it was again removed to Durham, where it remained for several centuries.

The second MS. is called the Rushworth MS., as it was presented to the Bodleian Library (Oxford) by John Rushworth, who was deputy-clerk to the House of Commons during the Long Parliament. The Latin text was written, probably in the eighth century, by a scribe named Macregol. The gloss, written in the latter half of the tenth century, is in two hands, those of Farman and Owun, whose names are given. Farman was a priest of Harewood, on the river Wharfe, in the West Riding of Yorkshire. He glossed the whole of St Matthew's Gospel, and a very small portion of St Mark. It is worthy of especial notice, that his gloss, throughout St Matthew, is not in the Northumbrian dialect, but in a form of Mercian. But it is clear that when he had completed this first Gospel, he borrowed the Lindisfarne MS. as a guide to help him, and kept it before him when he began to gloss St Mark. He at once began to copy the glosses in the older MS., with slight occasional variations in the grammar; but he soon tired of his task, and turned it over to Owun, who continued it to the end. The result is that the Northumbrian glosses in this MS., throughout the three last Gospels, are of no great value, as they tell us little more than can be better learnt from the Durham book; on the other hand, Farman's Mercian gloss to St Matthew is of high value, but need not be considered at present. Hence it is best in this case to rely, for our knowledge of Old Northumbrian, on the Durham book *alone*.

It must be remembered that a gloss is not quite the same thing as a free translation that observes the rules of grammar. A gloss translates the Latin text word by word, in the order of that text; so that the glossator can neither observe the natural English order nor in all cases preserve the English grammar;

a fact which somewhat lessens its value, and must always be allowed for. It is therefore necessary, in all cases, to ascertain the Latin text. I subjoin a specimen, from Matt. v 11—15.

eadge aron ge mith thy yfle hia gecuoethas iuh and mith thy
11. Beati estis cum maledixerunt uobis et cum per-
oehtas iuih and cuoethas eghwelc yfel with iuih
secuti uos fuerint et dixerint omne malum aduersum uos
gesuicas *vel* wæges fore mec gefeath and wynnsumiath forthon
mentientes propter me. 12. gaudete et exultate quoniam
mearda iuere monigfalde is *vel* sint in heofnum suæ *vel* suelce ec forthon
merces uestra copiosa est in caelis sic enim
ge-oehton tha witgo tha the weron ær iuih gee
persecuti sunt prophetas qui fuerunt ante uos. 13. Uos
sint salt eorthes thæt gif salt forworthes in thon gesælted bith to
estis sal terrae quod si sal euanuerit in quo sallietur ad
nowihte *vel* nænihte mæge ofer thæt buta thæt gesended bith *vel* geworpen út
nihilum ualet ultra nisi ut mittatur foras
and getreden bith from monnum gie aron *vel* sint leht middangeardes
et conculcetur ab hominibus 14. Uos estis lux mundi
ne mæg burug *vel* ceastra gehyda *vel* gedeigla ofer mor geseted
non potest ciuitas abscondi supra monte posita.
ne ec bernas thæccillo *vel* leht-fæt and settas tha *vel* hia unther mitte
15. neque accendunt lucernam et ponunt eam sub
vel under sestre ah ofer leht-isern and lihteth allum tha the in
modio sed super candelabrum et luceat omnibus qui in
hus bithon *vel* sint
domo sunt.

The history of the Northern dialect during the next three centuries, from the year 1000 to nearly 1300, with a few insignificant exceptions, is a total blank.

CHAPTER IV

THE DIALECTS OF NORTHUMBRIA; A.D. 1300–1400

A LITTLE before 1300, we come to a *Metrical English Psalter*, published by the Surtees Society in 1843–7. The language is supposed to represent the speech of Yorkshire. It is translated (rather closely) from the Latin Vulgate version. I give a specimen from Psalm xviii, 14—20.

14. He sent his arwes, and skatered tha;
Felefalded levening, and dreved tham swa.
15. And schewed welles of watres ware,
And groundes of ertheli werld unhiled are,
For thi snibbing, Laverd myne;
For onesprute of gast of wreth thine.
16. He sent fra hegh, and uptoke me;
Fra many watres me nam he.
17. He out-toke me thare amang
Fra my faas that war sa strang,
And fra tha me that hated ai;
For samen strenghthed over me war thai.
18. Thai forcome me in daie of twinging,
And made es Lavered mi forhiling.
19. And he led me in brede to be;
Sauf made he me, for he wald me;

20. And foryhelde to me Laverd sal
After mi rightwisenes al.
And after clensing of mi hende
Sal he yhelde to me at ende.

The literal sense is:—"He sent His arrows and scattered them; multiplied (His) lightning and so afflicted them. And the wells of waters were shown, and the foundations of the earthly world are uncovered because of Thy snubbing (rebuke), O my Lord! because of the blast (Lat. *inspiratio*) of the breath of Thy wrath. He sent from on high, and took me up; from many waters He took me. He took me out there-among from my foes that were so strong, and from those that alway hated me; for they were strengthened together over me. They came before me in the day of affliction, and the Lord is made my protection. And He led me (so as) to be in a broad place; He made me safe, because He desired (lit. would) me; and the Lord shall requite me according to all my righteousness, and according to the cleanness of my hands shall He repay me in the end."

In this specimen we can already discern some of the chief characteristics which are so conspicuous in Lowland Scotch MSS. of the fourteenth and fifteenth centuries. The most striking is the almost total loss of the final *-e* which is so frequently required to form an extra syllable when we try to scan the poetry of

Chaucer. Even where a final *-e* is written in the above extract, it is wholly silent. The words *ware* (were), *are* (are), *myne, thine, toke, made, brede, hende, ende,* are all monosyllabic; and in fact the large number of monosyllabic words is very striking. The words *onesprute, forcome, foryhelde* are, in like manner, dissyllabic. The only suffixes that count in the scansion are *-en, -ed,* and *-es*; as in *sam-en, skat'r-èd, drev-èd, hat-èd,* etc., and *arw-ès, well-ès, watr-ès,* etc. The curious form *sal,* for "shall," is a Northern characteristic. So also is the form *hende* as the plural of "hand"; the Southern plural was often *hond-en,* and the Midland form was *hond-ès* or *hand-ès.* Note also the characteristic long *a*; as in *swa* for *swo,* so; *gast,* ghost; *fra,* fro; *faas,* foes. It was pronounced like the *a* in *father.*

A much longer specimen of the *Metrical English Psalter* will be found in *Specimens of Early English,* ed. Morris and Skeat, Part II, pp. 23—34, and is easily accessible. In the same volume, the Specimens numbered VII, VIII, X, XI, and XVI are also in Northumbrian, and can easily be examined. It will therefore suffice to give a very brief account of each.

VII. *Cursor Mundi,* or *Cursor o Werld,* i.e. Over-runner of the World; so called because it rehearses a great part of the world's history, from the creation onwards. It is a poem of portentous length, extending to 29,555 lines, and recounts many of the events found in the Old and New Testaments, with the addition of legends from many other sources, one of them, for example, being the *Historia Scholastica* of Peter Comestor. Dr Murray thinks it may have been written in the neighbourhood of Durham. The specimen given (pp. 69—82) corresponds to lines 11373—11796.

VIII. *Sunday Homilies in Verse*; about 1330. The extracts are taken from *English Metrical Homilies*, edited by J. Small (Edinburgh, 1862) from a MS. in Edinburgh. The Northern dialect is well marked, but I do not know to what locality to assign it.

X. Richard Rolle, of Hampole, near Doncaster, wrote a poem called *The Prick of Conscience*, about 1340. It extends to 9624 lines, and was edited by Dr Morris for the Philological Society in 1863. The Preface to this edition is of especial value, as it carefully describes the characteristics of Northumbrian, and practically laid the foundation of our knowledge of the old dialects as exhibited in MSS. Lists are given of orthographical differences between the Northern dialect and others, and an analysis is added giving the grammatical details which determine its Northern character. Much of this information is repeated in the Introduction to the *Specimens of English*, Part II, pp. xviii—xxxviii.

XI. *The Poems of Laurence Minot* belong to the middle of the fourteenth century. He composed eleven poems in celebration of events that occurred between the years 1333 and 1352. They were first printed by Ritson in 1795; and subsequently by T. Wright, in his *Political Poems and Songs* (London, 1859); and are now very accessible in the excellent and cheap (second) edition by Joseph Hall (Oxford University Press). There is also a German edition by Dr Wilhelm Scholle. The poet seems to have been connected with Yorkshire, and the dialect is not purely Northern, as it shows a slight admixture of Midland forms.

XVI. *The Bruce*; by John Barbour; partly written in 1375. It has been frequently printed, viz. in 1616, 1620, 1670, 1672, 1715, 1737, and 1758; and was edited by Pinkerton in 1790, by Jamieson in 1820, and by Cosmo Innes in 1866; also by myself (for the Early English Text Society) in 1870–89; and again (for the Scottish Text Society) in 1893–5. Unfortunately, the two extant MSS. were both written out about a century after the date of composition. Nevertheless, we have the text of more than 260 lines as it existed in 1440, as this portion was quoted by Andro of Wyntown, in his *Cronykil of Scotland*, written at that date. I quote some lines from this portion, taken from *The Bruce*, Book i, 37—56, 91—110; with a few explanations in the footnotes.

Qwhen Alysandyre oure kyng wes dede,
That Scotland had to stere[1] and lede,
The land sex yhere and mayr perfay[2]
Wes desolate efftyr his day.
The barnage[3] off Scotland, at the last,
Assemblyd thame, and fandyt[4] fast
To chess[5] a kyng, thare land to stere,
That off awncestry cummyn were
Off kyngis that aucht[6] that reawté[7],
And mast[8] had rycht thare kyng to be.
But inwy[9], that is sa fellowne[10],
Amang thame mad dissensiown:
For sum wald have the Ballyolle kyng,
For he wes cumyn off that ofspryng
That off the eldest systere was;
And other sum nyt[11] all that cas,
And sayd, that he thare kyng suld be,
That wes in als nere[12] degre,
And cummyn wes off the nerrast male
In thai[13] brawnchys collateralle...
A! blynd folk, fulle off all foly,
Had yhe wmbethowcht[14] yowe inkkyrly[15]
Quhat peryle to yowe mycht appere,
Yhe had noucht wroucht on this manèr.
Had yhe tane kepe[16], how that that kyng
Off Walys, forowtyn sudiowrnyng[17],
Trawaylyd[18] to wyn the senyhowry[19],
And throw his mycht till occupy
Landys, that ware till hym marchand[20],

[1] *govern* [2] *more, by my faith* [3] *nobility* [4] *endeavoured* [5] *choose* [6] *possessed* [7] *royalty* [8] *most* [9] *envy* [10] *wicked* [11] *others denied* [12] *as near* [13] *those* [14] *bethought* [15] *especially* [16] *taken heed* [17] *without delay* [18] *laboured* [19] *sovereignty* [20] *bordering*

As Walys was, and als Irland,
That he put till sic threllage[21],
That thai, that ware off hey parage[22],
Suld ryn on fwte, as rybalddale[23],
Quhen ony folk he wald assale.
Durst nane of Walis in batale ryd,
Na yhit, fra evyn fell[24], abyde
Castell or wallyd towne within,
Than[25] he suld lyff and lymmys tyne[26].
Into swylk thryllage[27] thame held he
That he owre-come with his powsté[28].

In this extract, as in that from the *Metrical Psalter* above, there is a striking preponderance of monosyllables, and, as in that case also, the final *-e* is invariably silent in such words as *oure, stere, lede, yhere, thare, were,* etc., just as in modern English. The grammar is, for the most part, extremely simple, as at the present day. The chief difficulty lies in the vocabulary, which contains some words that are either obsolete or provincial. Many of the obsolete words are found in other dialects; thus *stere,* to control, *perfay, fonden* (for *fanden*), *chesen,* to choose, *feloun,* adj. meaning "angry," *take kepe, soiourne,* to tarry, *travaile,* to labour, *parage,* rank, all occur in Chaucer; *barnage, reauté,* in *William of Palerne* (in the Midland dialect, possibly Shropshire); *oughte,* owned, possessed, *tyne,* to lose, in *Piers the Plowman*; *um-*

[21] *such subjection* [22] *high rank* [23] *rabble* [24] *after evening fell*
[25] *but* [26] *lose* [27] *thraldom* [28] *power*

bethinken, in the *Ormulum*; *enkerly* (for *inkkyrly*), in the alliterative *Morte Arthure*; *march*, to border upon, in *Mandeville*; *seignorie*, in *Robert of Gloucester*. Barbour is rather fond of introducing French words; *rybalddale* occurs in no other author. *Threllage* or *thryllage* may have been coined from *threll* (English *thrall*), by adding a French suffix. As to the difficult word *nyt*, see *Nite* in the *N.E.D.*

In addition to the poems, etc., already mentioned, further material may be found in the prose works of Richard Rolle of Hampole, especially his translation and exposition of the Psalter, edited by the Rev. H. R. Bramley (Oxford, 1884), and the Prose Treatises edited by the Rev. G. G. Perry for the Early English Text Society. Dr Murray further calls attention to the Early Scottish Laws, of which the vernacular translations partly belong to the fourteenth century.

I have now mentioned the chief authorities for the study of the Northern dialect from early times down to 1400. Examination of them leads directly to a result but little known, and one that is in direct contradiction to general uninstructed opinion; namely that, down to this date, the varieties of Northumbrian are much fewer and slighter than they afterwards became, and that the written documents are practically all in one and the same dialect, or very nearly so, from the Humber as far north as Aberdeen. The irrefragable results noted by Dr Murray will probably come as a surprise to many, though they have now been before the public for more than forty years. The Durham dialect of the *Cursor Mundi* and the Aberdeen Scotch of Barbour are hardly distinguishable by grammatical or orthographical tests; and both bear a remarkable resemblance to the Yorkshire dialect as found in Hampole. What is now called Lowland Scotch is so nearly descended from the Old Northumbrian that the latter was invariably called "Ingliss" by the writers who employed it; and they reserved the name of "Scottish" to designate Gaelic or Erse, the tongue of the original "Scots," who gave their name to the country. Barbour (*Bruce*, IV 253) calls his own language "Ynglis." Andro of Wyntown does the same, near the beginning of the Prologue to his *Cronykil*. The most striking case is that of Harry the Minstrel, who was so opposed to all Englanders, from a political point of view, that his whole poem breathes fury and hatred against them; and yet, in describing Wallace's French friend, Longueville, who knew no tongue but his own, he says of him (*Wallace*, IX 295–7):

> Lykly he was, manlik of contenance,
> *Lik to the Scottis* be mekill governance
> *Saiff off his tong*, for *Inglis* had he nane.

Later still, Dunbar, near the conclusion of his *Golden Targe*, apostrophises Chaucer as being "in *oure Tong* ane flouir imperiall," and says that he was "*of oure Inglisch* all the lycht." It was not till 1513 that Gawain Douglas, in the Prologue to the first book of his translation of Virgil, claimed to have "writtin in the langage of Scottis natioun"; though Sir David Lyndesay, writing twenty-two years later, still gives the name of the "Inglisch toung" to the vulgar tongue of Scotland, in his *Satyre of the three Estaitis.*

We should particularly notice Dr Murray's statement, in his essay on *The Dialect of the Southern Counties of Scotland,* at p. 29, that "Barbour at Aberdeen, and Richard Rolle de Hampole near Doncaster, wrote for their several countrymen in the same identical dialect." The division between the English of the Scottish Lowlands and the English of Yorkshire was purely political, having no reference to race or speech, but solely to locality; and yet, as Dr Murray remarks, the struggle for supremacy "made every one either an Englishman or a Scotchman, and made English and Scotch names of division and bitter enmity." So strong, indeed, was the division thus created that it has continued to the present day; and it would be very difficult even now to convince a native of the Scottish Lowlands—unless he is a philologist—that he is likely to be of Anglian descent, and to have a better title to be called an "Englishman" than a native of Hampshire or Devon, who, after all, may be only a Saxon. And of course it is easy enough to show how widely the old "Northern" dialect varies from the difficult Southern English found in the Kentish *Ayenbite of Inwyt*, or even from the Midland of Chaucer's poems.

To quote from Dr Murray once more (p. 41): "the facts are still far from being generally known, and I have repeatedly been amused, on reading passages from *Cursor Mundi* and Hampole to men of education, both English and Scotch, to hear them all pronounce the dialect 'Old Scotch.' Great has been the surprise of the latter especially on being told that Richard the Hermit [i.e. of Hampole] wrote in the extreme south of Yorkshire, within a few miles of a locality so thoroughly English as Sherwood Forest, with its memories of Robin Hood. Such is the difficulty which people have in separating the natural and ethnological relations in which national names originate from the accidental values which they acquire through political complications and the fortunes of crowns and dynasties, that oftener than once the protest has been made—'Then he must have been a Scotchman settled there!'" The retort is obvious enough, that Barbour and Henry the Minstrel and Dunbar and Lyndesay have all recorded that their native language was "Inglis" or "Inglisch"; and it is interesting to note that, having regard to the pronunciation, they seem to have known, better than we do, how that name ought to be spelt.

CHAPTER V

NORTHUMBRIAN IN THE FIFTEENTH CENTURY

THE subject of the last chapter was one of great importance. When it is once understood that, down to 1400 or a little later, the men of the Scottish Lowlands and the men of the northern part of England spoke not only the same language, but the same dialect of that language, it becomes easy to explain what happened afterwards.

There was, nevertheless, one profound difference between the circumstances of the language spoken to the north of the Tweed and that spoken to the south of it. In Scotland, the Northumbrian dialect was spoken by all but the Celts, without much variety; the minor differences need not be here considered. And this dialect, called Inglis (as we have seen) by the Lowlanders themselves, had no rival, as the difference between it and the Erse or Gaelic was obvious and immutable.

To the South of the Tweed, the case was different. England already possessed three dialects at least, viz. Northumbrian, Mercian, and Saxon, i.e. Northern,

Midland, and Southern; besides which, Midland had at the least two main varieties, viz. Eastern and Western. Between all these there was a long contention for supremacy. In very early days, the Northern took the lead, but its literature was practically destroyed by the Danes, and it never afterwards attained to anything higher than a second place. From the time of Alfred, the standard language of literature was the Southern, and it kept the lead till long after the Conquest, well down to 1200 and even later, as will be explained hereafter. But the Midland dialect, which is not without witness to its value in the ninth century, began in the thirteenth to assume an important position, which in the fourteenth became dominant and supreme, exalted as it was by the genius of Chaucer. Its use was really founded on practical convenience. It was intermediate between the other two, and could be more or less comprehended both by the Northerner and the Southerner, though these could hardly understand each other. The result was, naturally, that whilst the Northumbrian to the north of the Tweed was practically supreme, the Northumbrian to the south of it soon lost its position as a literary medium. It thus becomes clear that we must, during the fifteenth century, treat the Northumbrian of England and that of Scotland separately. Let us first investigate its position in England.

But before this can be appreciated, it is necessary to draw attention to the fact that the literature of the fifteenth century, in nearly all the text-books that treat of the subject, has been most unjustly underrated. The critics, nearly all with one accord, repeat the remark that it is a "barren" period, with nothing admirable about it, at any rate in England; that it shows us the works of Hoccleve and Lydgate near the beginning, *The Flower and the Leaf* near the middle (about 1460), and the ballad of *The Nut-brown Maid* at the end of it, and nothing else that is remarkable. In other words, they neglect its most important characteristic, that it was the chief period of the lengthy popular romances and of the popular plays out of which the great dramas of the succeeding century took their rise. To which it deserves to be added that it contains many short poems of a fugitive character, whilst a vast number of very popular ballads were in constant vogue, sometimes handed down without much change by a faithful tradition, but more frequently varied by the fancy of the more competent among the numerous wandering minstrels. To omit from the fifteenth century nearly all account of its romances and plays and ballads is like omitting the part of Hamlet the Dane from Shakespeare's greatest tragedy.

The passion for long romances or romantic poems had already arisen in the fourteenth century, and, to some extent, in the thirteenth. Even just before 1300, we meet with the lays of *Havelok* and *Horn*. In the fourteenth century, it is sufficient to mention the romances of *Sir Guy of Warwick* (the earlier version), *Sir Bevis of Hamtoun*, and *Libeaus Desconus*, all mentioned by Chaucer; *Sir Launfal*, *The Seven Sages* (earlier version, as edited by Weber); *Lai le Freine*, *Richard Coer de Lion*, *Amis and Amiloun*, *The King of Tars*, *William of Palerne*, *Joseph of Arimathea* (a fragment), *Sir Gawain and the Grene Knight*, *Alisaunder of Macedoine* and *Alexander and Dindimus* (two fragments of one very long poem), *Sir Ferumbras*, and *Sir Isumbras*. The spirited romance generally known as the alliterative *Morte Arthure* must also belong here, though the MS. itself is of later date.

The series was actively continued during the fifteenth century, when we find, besides others, the romances of *Iwain and Gawain*, *Sir Percival*, and *Sir Cleges*; *The Sowdon* (Sultan) *of Babylon*; *The Aunturs* (Adventures) *of Arthur*, *Sir Amadas*, *The Avowing of Arthur*, and *The Life of Ipomidoun*; *The Wars of Alexander*, *The Seven Sages* (later version, edited by Wright); *Torrent of Portugal*, *Sir Gowther*, *Sir Degrevant*, *Sir Eglamour*, *Le Bone Florence of Rome*, and *Partonope of Blois*; the prose version of *Merlin*, the later version of *Sir Guy of Warwick*, and the verse Romance, of immense length, of *The Holy Grail; Emare, The Erl of Tolous,* and *The Squire of Low Degree.* Towards the end of the century, when the printing-press was already at work, we find Caxton greatly busying himself to continue the list. Not only did he give us the whole of Sir Thomas Malory's *Morte D'Arthur,* "enprynted and fynysshed in thabbey Westmestre the last day of Iuyl, the yere of our lord MCCCCLXXXV"; but he actually translated several romances into very good English prose on his own account, viz. *Godefroy of Boloyne* (1481), *Charles the Grete* (1485), *The Knight Paris and the fair Vyene* (1485), *Blanchardyn and Eglantine* (about 1489), and *The Four Sons of Aymon* (about 1490). We must further put to the credit of the fifteenth century the remarkable English version of the *Gesta Romanorum,* and many more versions by Caxton, such as *The Recuyell of the Historyes of Troye, The Life of Jason, Eneydos* (which is Virgil's *Æneid* in the form of a prose romance), *The Golden Legend* or Lives of Saints, and *Reynard the Fox.* When all these works are considered, the fifteenth century emerges with considerable credit.

It remains to look at some of the above-named romances a little more closely, in order to see if any of them are in the dialect of Northern England. Some of them are written by scribes belonging to other parts, but there seems to be little doubt that the following were in that dialect originally, viz. (1) *Iwain and Gawain*, printed in Ritson's *Ancient Metrical Romances*, and belonging to the very beginning of the century, extant in the same MS. as that which contains Minot's *Poems*: (2) *The Wars of Alexander* (Early English Text Society, 1886), edited by myself; see the Preface, pp. xv, xix, for proofs that it was originally written in a pure Northumbrian dialect, which the better of the two MSS. very fairly preserves. Others exhibit strong traces of a Northern dialect, such as *The Aunturs of Arthur*, *Sir Amadas*, and *The Avowing of Arthur*, but they may be in a West Midland dialect, not far removed from the North. In the preface to *The Sege of Melayne* (Milan) *and Roland and Otuel*, edited for the Early English Text Society by S. J. Herrtage, it is suggested that both these poems were by the author of *Sir Percival*, and that all three were originally in the dialect of the North of England.

Iwain and Gawain and *The Wars of Alexander* belong to quite the beginning of the fifteenth century, and they appear to be among the latest examples of the literary use of dialect in the North of England considered as a vehicle for romances; but we must not forget the "miracle plays," and in particular *The Towneley Mysteries* or plays acted at or near Wakefield in Yorkshire, and *The York Plays*, lately edited by Miss Toulmin Smith. Examples of Southern

English likewise come to an end about the same time; it is most remarkable how very soon, after the death of Chaucer, the Midland dialect not only assumed a leading position, but enjoyed that proud position almost alone. The rapid loss of numerous inflexions, soon after 1400, made that dialect, which was already in possession of such important centres as London, Oxford, and Cambridge, much easier to learn, and brought its grammar much nearer to that in use in the North. It even compromised, as it were, with that dialect by accepting from it the general use of such important words as *they*, *their*, *them*, the plural verb *are*, and the preposition *till*. There can be little doubt that one of the causes of the cessation of varying forms of words in literary use was the civil strife known as the Wars of the Roses, which must for a brief period have been hostile to all literary activity; and very shortly afterwards the printing-presses of London all combined to recognise, in general, one dialect only.

Hence it came about, by a natural but somewhat rapid process, that the only dialect which remained unaffected by the triumph of the Midland variety was that portion of the Northern dialect which still held its own in Scotland, where it was spoken by subjects of another king. As far as literature was concerned, only two dialects were available, the Northumbrian of Scotland and the East Midland in

England. It is obvious that the readiest way of distinguishing between the two is to call the one "Scottish" and the other "English," ignoring accuracy for the sake of practical convenience. This is precisely what happened in course of time, and the new nomenclature would have done no harm if the study of Middle English had been at all general. But such was not the case, and the history of our literature was so much neglected that even those who should have been well informed knew no better than others. The chief modern example is the well-known case of that most important and valuable book entitled *An Etymological Dictionary of the Scottish Language*, by John Jamieson, D.D., first published in Edinburgh in 1808. There is no great harm in the title, if for "Language" we read "Dialect"; but this great and monumental work was unluckily preceded by a "Dissertation on the Origin of the Scottish Language," in which wholly mistaken and wrongheaded views are supported with great ingenuity and much show of learning. In the admirable new edition of "Jamieson" by Longmuir and Donaldson, published at Paisley in 1879, this matter is set right. They quite rightly reprint this "Dissertation," which affords valuable testimony as to the study of English in 1808, but accompany it with most judicious remarks, which are well worthy of full repetition. "That once famous Dissertation can now be considered only a notable feat of literary card-building; more remarkable for the skill and ingenuity of its construction than for its architectural correctness, strength and durability, or practical usefulness. That the language of the Scottish Lowlands is in all important particulars the same as that of the northern counties of England, will be evident to any unbiassed reader who takes the trouble to compare the Scottish Dictionary with the Glossaries of Brockett, Atkinson, and Peacock. And the similarity is attested in another way by the simple but important fact, that regarding some of our Northern Metrical Romances it is still disputed whether they were composed to the north or the south of the Tweed....And to this conclusion all competent scholars have given their consent."

For those who really understand the situation there is no harm in accepting the distinction between "Scottish" and "English," as explained above. Hence it is that the name of "Middle Scots" has been suggested for "the literary language of Scotland written between the latter half of the fifteenth century and the early decades of the seventeenth." Most of this literature is highly interesting, at any rate much more so than the "English" literature of the same period, as has been repeatedly remarked. Indeed, this is so well known that special examples are needless; I content myself with referring to the *Specimens of Middle Scots*, by G. Gregory Smith, Edinburgh and London, 1902. These specimens include extracts from such famous authors as Henryson, Dunbar, Gawain (or Gavin) Douglas, Sir David Lyndesay, John Knox, and George Buchanan. Perhaps it is well to add that "Scottis" or "Scots" is the Northern form of "Scottish" or "Scotch"; just as "Inglis" is the Northern form of "English."

"Middle Scots" implies both "Old Scots" and "Modern Scots." "Old Scots" is, of course, the same thing as Northumbrian or Northern English of the Middle English Period, which may be roughly dated as extant from 1300 to 1400 or 1450. "Modern Scots" is the dialect (when they employ dialect) illustrated by Allan Ramsay, Alexander Ross, Robert Tannahill, John Galt, James Hogg (the Ettrick Shepherd), Robert Burns, Sir Walter Scott, and very many others.

I conclude this chapter with a characteristic example of Middle Scots. The following well-known passage is from the conclusion to Dunbar's *Golden Targe.*

And as I did awake of my sweving[1],
The ioyfull birdis merily did syng
  For myrth of Phebus tendir bemës schene[2];
Swete war the vapouris, soft the morowing[3],
Halesum the vale, depaynt wyth flouris ying[4];
  The air attemperit, sobir, and amene[5];
  In quhite and rede was all the feld besene[6]

[1] *dream* [2] *bright* [3] *morn* [4] *young* [5] *pleasant* [6] *arrayed*

Throu Naturis nobil fresch anamalyng[7],
  In mirthfull May, of eviry moneth Quene.

O reverend Chaucere, rose of rethoris[8] all,
As in oure tong ane flour[9] imperiall,
  That raise[10] in Britane evir, quho redis rycht,
Thou beris of makaris[11] the tryúmph riall;
Thy fresch anamalit termës celicall[12]
  This mater coud illumynit have full brycht;
  Was thou noucht of oure Inglisch all the lycht,
Surmounting eviry tong terrestriall
  Als fer as Mayis morow dois mydnycht?

O morall Gower, and Ludgate laureate,
Your sugurit lippis and tongis aureate[13]
  Bene to oure eris cause of grete delyte;
Your angel mouthis most mellifluate[14]
Oure rude langage has clere illumynate,
  And faire our-gilt[15] oure speche, that imperfýte
  Stude, or[16] your goldyn pennis schupe[17] to wryte;
This ile before was bare, and desolate
  Of rethorike, or lusty[18] fresch endyte[19].

[7] *enamelling* [8] *orators* [9] *flower* [10] *didst rise* [11] *poets*
[12] *heavenly* [13] *golden* [14] *honeyed* [15] *overgilt* [16] *ere*
[17] *undertook* [18] *pleasant* [19] *composition*

CHAPTER VI

THE SOUTHERN DIALECT

WE have seen that the earliest dialect to assume literary supremacy was the Northern, and that at a very early date, namely, in the seventh, eighth, and ninth centuries; but its early documents have nearly all perished. If, with the exception of one short fragment, any of Cædmon's poems have survived, they only exist in Southern versions of a much later date.

The chief fosterer of our rather extensive Wessex (or Southern) literature, commonly called Anglo-Saxon, was the great Alfred, born at Wantage in Berkshire, to the south of the Thames. We may roughly define the limits of the Old Southern dialect by saying that it formerly included all the counties to the south of the Thames and to the west and south-west of Berkshire, including Wiltshire, Dorsetshire, Somersetshire, and Devonshire, but excluding Cornwall, in which the Cornish dialect of Celtic prevailed. It was at Athelney in Somersetshire, near the junction of the rivers Tone and Parrett, that Alfred, in the memorable year 878, when his dominions were reduced to a precarious sway over two or three counties, established his famous stronghold; from which he issued to inflict upon the foes of the future British empire a crushing and decisive defeat. And it was near Athelney, in the year 1693, that the ornament of gold and enamel was found, with its famous legend—ÆLFRED MEC HEHT GEWYRCAN—"Ælfred commanded (men) to make me."

From his date to the Norman Conquest, the MSS. in the Anglo-Saxon or Southern dialect are fairly numerous, and it is mainly to them that we owe our knowledge of the grammar, the metre, and the pronunciation of the older forms of English. Sweet's *Anglo-Saxon Primer* will enable any one to begin the study of this dialect, and to learn something valuable about it in the course of a month or two.

The famous *Anglo-Saxon Chronicle*, beginning with a note concerning the year 1, when Augustus was emperor of Rome, not only continues our history down to the Conquest, but for nearly a century beyond it, to the year 1154. The language of the latter part, as extant in the (Midland) Laud MS., belongs to the twelfth century, and shows considerable changes in the spelling and grammar as compared with the Parker MS., which (not counting in a few later entries) ends with the year 1001.

After the Conquest, the Southern dialect continued

to be the literary language, and we have several examples of it. Extracts from some of the chief works are given in Part I of Morris's *Specimens of Early English*. They are selected from the following: (1) *Old English Homilies*, 1150—1200, as printed for the Early English Text Society, and edited by Dr Morris, 1867–8. (2) *Old English Homilies, Second Series*, before 1200, ed. Morris (E.E.T.S.), 1873. (3) *The Brut*, being a versified chronicle of the legendary history of Britain, compiled by Layamon, a Worcestershire priest, and extending to 32,240 (short) lines; in two versions, the date of the earlier being about 1205. (4) *A Life of St Juliana*, in two versions, about 1210; ed. Cockayne and Brock (E.E.T.S.), 1872. (5) *The Ancren Riwle*, or Rule of anchorite nuns (Camden Society), ed. Morton, 1853; the date of composition is about 1210. (6) *The Proverbs of Alfred*, about 1250; printed in Dr Morris's *Old English Miscellany* (E.E.T.S.), 1872. A later edition, by myself, was printed at Oxford in 1907. (7) A poem by Nicholas de Guildford, entitled *The Owl and the Nightingale*, about 1250; ed. Rev. J. Stevenson, 1838; ed. T. Wright, 1843; ed. F. H. Stratmann, of Krefeld, 1868. (8) A curious poem of nearly 400 long lines, usually known as *A Moral Ode*, which seems to have been originally written at Christchurch, Hampshire, and frequently printed; one version is in Morris's *Old English Homilies*, and another in the

Second Series of the same. (9) *The Romance of King Horn*; before 1300, here printed in full.

Just at the very end of the century we meet with two Southern poems of vast length. *The Metrical Chronicle* of Robert of Gloucester, comprising the History of Britain from the Siege of Troy to the year 1272, the date of the accession of Edward I, and written in the dialect of Gloucester, was completed in 1298. It must seem strange to many to find that our history is thus connected with the Siege of Troy; but it must be remembered that our old histories, including Layamon's poem of *The Brut* mentioned above, usually included the fabulous history of very early Britain as narrated by Geoffrey of Monmouth; and it is useful to remember that we owe to this circumstance such important works as Shakespeare's *King Lear* and *Cymbeline*, as well as the old play of *Locrine*, once attributed to Shakespeare. According to Robert's version of Geoffrey's story, Britain was originally called Brutain, after Brut or Brutus, the son of Æneas. Locrin was the eldest son of Brutus and his wife Innogen, and defeated Humber, king of Hungary, in a great battle; after which Humber was drowned in the river which still bears his name. Locrin's daughter Averne (or Sabre in Geoffrey) was drowned likewise, in the river which was consequently called Severn. The British king Bathulf (or, in Geoffrey, Bladud) was the builder of Bath; and the son of Bladud was Leir, who had three daughters, named Gornorille, Regan, and Cordeille. Kymbel (in Geoffrey, Kymbelinus), who had been brought up by Augustus Cæsar, was king of Britain at the time of the birth of Christ; his sons were Guider and Arvirag (Guiderius and Arviragus). Another king of Britain was King Cole, who gave name (says Geoffrey falsely) to Colchester. We come into touch with authentic history with the reign of Vortigern, when Hengist and Horsa sailed over to Britain. An extract from Robert of Gloucester is given in *Specimens of Early English*, Part II.

The other great work of the same date is the vast collection edited for the Early English Text Society by Dr Horstmann in 1887, entitled, *The Early South-English Legendary*, or Lives of Saints. It is extant in several MSS., of which the oldest (MS. Laud 108) originally contained 67 Lives; with an Appendix, in a later hand, containing two more. The eleventh Life is that of St Dunstan, which is printed in *Specimens of Early English*, Part II, from another MS.

Soon after the year 1300 the use of the Southern dialect becomes much less frequent, with the exception of such pieces as belong particularly to the county of Kent and will be considered by themselves. There are two immense manuscript collections of various poems, originally in various dialects, which are worth notice. One of these is the Harleian MS. No. 2253, in the British Museum, the scribe of which has reduced everything into the South-Western dialect, though it is plain that, in many cases, it is not the dialect in which the pieces were originally composed; this famous manuscript belongs to the beginning of the fourteenth century. Many poems were printed from it, with the title of *Altenglische Dichtungen*, by Dr K. Böddeker, in 1878. Another similar collection is contained in the Vernon MS. at Oxford, and belongs to the very end of the same century; the poems in it are all in a Southern dialect, which is that of the scribe. It contains, e.g., a copy of the earliest version of *Piers the Plowman*, which would have been far more valuable if the scribe had retained the spelling of his copy. This may help us to realise one of the great difficulties which beset the study of dialects, namely, that we usually find copies of old poems reduced to the scribe's *own* dialect; and it may easily happen that such a copy varies considerably from the correct form.

It has already been shown that the rapid rise and spread of the Midland dialect during the fourteenth century practically put an end to the literary use of Northern not long after 1400, except in Scotland. It affected Southern in the same way, but at a somewhat earlier date; so that (even in Kent) it is very difficult to find a Southern work after 1350. There is, however, one remarkable exception in the case of a work which may be dated in 1387, written by John Trevisa. Trevisa (as the prefix Tre- suggests) was a native of Cornwall, but he resided chiefly in Gloucestershire, where he was vicar of Berkeley, and chaplain to Thomas Lord Berkeley. The work to which I here refer is known as his translation of Higden. Ralph Higden, a Benedictine monk in the Abbey of St Werburg at Chester, wrote in Latin a long history of the world in general, and of Britain in particular, with the title of the *Polychronicon*, which achieved considerable popularity. The first book of this history contains 60 chapters, the first of which begins with P, the second with R, and so on. If all these initials are copied out in their actual order, we obtain a complete sentence, as follows:—"Presentem cronicam compilavit Frater Ranulphus Cestrensis monachus"; i.e. Brother Ralph, monk of Chester, compiled the present chronicle. I mention this curious device on the part of Higden because another similar acrostic occurs elsewhere. It so happens that Higden's *Polychronicon* was continued, after his death, by John Malverne, who brought down the history to a later date, and included in it an account of a certain Thomas Usk, with whom he seems to have been acquainted. Now, in a lengthy prose work of about 1387, called *The Testament of Love*, I one day discovered that its author had adopted a similar device—no doubt imitating Higden—and had so arranged that the initial letters of his chapters should form a sentence, as follows:—"Margarete of virtw, have merci on Thsknvi." There is no difficulty about the expression "Margarete of virtw," because the treatise itself explains that it means Holy Church, but I could make nothing of *Thsknvi*, as the letters evidently require rearrangement. But Mr Henry Bradley, one of the editors of the *New English Dictionary*, discovered that the chapters near the end of the treatise are out of order; and when he had restored sense by putting them as they should be, the new reading of the last seven letters came out as "thin vsk," i.e. "thine Usk"; and the attribution of this treatise to Thomas Usk clears up every difficulty and fits in with all that John Malverne says. This, in fact, is the happy solution of the authorship of *The Testament of Love*, which was once attributed to Chaucer, though it is obviously not his at all.

But it is time to return to John Trevisa, Higden's translator. This long translation is all in the Southern dialect, originally that of Gloucestershire, though there are several MSS. that do not always agree. A fair copy of it, from a MS. in the library of St John's College, Cambridge, is given side by side with the original Latin in the edition already noticed. It is worth adding that Caxton printed Trevisa's version, altering the spelling to suit that of his own time, and giving several variations of reading.

Trevisa was also the author of some other works, of which the most important is his translation into English, from the original Latin, of *Bartholomæus de Proprietatibus Rerum.*

I am not aware of any important work in the Southern dialect later than these translations by Trevisa. But in quite modern times, an excellent example of it has appeared, viz. in the *Poems of Rural Life, in the Dorset Dialect,* by William Barnes.

CHAPTER VII

THE SOUTHERN DIALECT OF KENT

THOUGH the Kentish dialect properly belongs to Southern English, from its position to the south of the Thames, yet it shows certain peculiarities which make it desirable to consider it apart from the rest.

In Beda's *Ecclesiastical History*, Bk I, ch. 15, he says of the Teutonic invaders: "Those who came over were of the three most powerful nations of Germany—Saxons, Angles, and Jutes. From the Jutes are descended the people of Kent, and of the Isle of Wight, and those also in the province of the West-Saxons who are to this day called Jutes, seated opposite to the Isle of Wight"; a remark which obviously implies the southern part of Hampshire. This suggests that the speech of Kent, from the very first, had peculiarities of its own. Dr Sweet, in his *Second Anglo-Saxon Reader, Archaic and Dialectal*, gives five very brief Kentish charters of the seventh and eighth centuries, but the texts are in Latin, and only the names of persons and places appear in Kentish forms. In the ninth century, however, there are seven Kentish charters, of a fuller description, from the year 805 to 837. In one of these, dated 835, a few lines occur that may be quoted:

Ic bidde and bebeode swælc monn se thæt min lond hebbe thæt he ælce gere agefe them higum æt Folcanstane l. ambra maltes, and vi. ambra gruta, and iii. wega spices and ceses, and cccc. hlafa, and an hrithr, and vi. scep....Thæm higum et Cristes cirican of thæm londe et Cealflocan: thæt is thonne thritig ombra alath, and threo hund hlafa, theara bith fiftig hwitehlafa, an weg spices and ceses, an ald hrithr, feower wedras, an suin oththe sex wedras, sex gosfuglas, ten hennfuglas, thritig teapera, gif hit wintres deg sie, sester fulne huniges, sester fulne butran, sester fulne saltes.

That is to say:

I ask and command, whosoever may have my land, that he every year give to the domestics at Folkestone fifty measures of malt, and six measures of meal, and three weys [*heavy weights*] of bacon and cheese, and four hundred loaves, and one rother [*ox*], and six sheep....To the domestics at Christ's church, from the land at Challock: that is, then, thirty vessels of ale, and three hundred loaves, of which fifty shall be white loaves, one wey of bacon and cheese, one old rother, four wethers, one swine or six wethers, six goose-fowls, ten hen-fowls, thirty tapers, if it be a day in winter, a jar full of honey, a jar full of butter, and a jar full of salt.

At pp. 152—175 of the same volume, Dr Sweet gives 1204 Kentish glosses of a very early date. No. 268 is: "*Cardines*, hearran"; and in several modern dialects, including Hampshire, the upright part of a gate to which the hinges are fastened is called a *harr*.

Several years ago, M. Paul Meyer found five short sermons in a Kentish dialect in MS. Laud 471, in the Bodleian Library, along with their French originals. They are printed in Morris's *Old English Miscellany*, and two of them will be found in *Specimens of Early English*, Part I, p. 141. The former of these is for the Epiphany, the text being taken from Matt. ii 1. The date is just before 1250. I give an extract.

Tho kinges hem wenten and hi seghen tho sterre thet yede bifore hem, alwat hi kam over tho huse war ure loverd was; and alswo hi hedden i-fonden ure loverd, swo hin an-urede, and him offrede hire offrendes, gold, and stor, and mirre. Tho nicht efter thet aperede an ongel of hevene in here slepe ine metinge, and hem seide and het, thet hi ne solde ayen wende be herodes, ac be an other weye wende into hire londes.

That is:

The kings went (them), and they saw the star that went before them until it came over the house where our Lord was; and as-soon-as they had found our Lord, so (they) honoured him, and offered him their offerings, gold, and frankincense, and myrrh. The night after that (there) appeared an angel from heaven in their sleep, in a dream, and said to-them and commanded, that they should not wend again near Herod, but by another way wend to their lands.

In the days of Edward II (1307–27) flourished William of Shoreham, named from Shoreham (Kent), near Otford and Sevenoaks, who was appointed vicar of Chart-Sutton in 1320. He translated the Psalter into English prose, and wrote some religious poems, chiefly relating to church-services, which were edited by T. Wright for the Percy Society in 1849. His poem "On Baptism" is printed in *Specimens of Early English*, Part II. I give an extract:

In water ich wel the cristny her[1]
  As Gode him-self hyt dightë[2];
For mide to wesschë[3] nis[4] nothynge
  That man cometh to so lightë[5]
      In londë[6];
Nis non that habben hit ne may[7]
  That habbe hit wilë foundë[8].

This bethe[9] the wordës of cristning
  By thyse Englísschë costës[10]—
"Ich[11] cristni the[12] ine the Vader[13] name
  And Sone and Holy Gostes"—
      And more,
"Amen!" wane hit[14] is ised[15] thertoe,
  Confermeth thet ther-to-fore[16].

In the year 1340, Dan Michel of Northgate (Kent) translated into English a French treatise on Vices and Virtues, under the title *The Ayenbite of Inwyt*, literally, "The Again-biting of In-wit," i.e. Remorse of Conscience. This is the best specimen of the Kentish dialect of the fourteenth century, and is

[1] *I desire thee to christen here* [2] *ordained it* [3] *to wash with* [4] *is not* [5] *easily* [6] *in (the) land* [7] *there is none that may not have it* [8] *that will try to have it* [9] *these are* [10] *coasts, regions* [11] *I* [12] *thee* [13] *Father's* [14] *when it* [15] *said* [16] *that which precedes*

remarkable for being much more difficult to make out than other pieces of the same period. The whole work was edited by Dr Morris for the Early English Text Society in 1866. A sermon of the same date and in the same dialect, and probably by the same author, is given in *Specimens of Early English*, Part II. The sermon is followed by the Lord's Prayer, the Ave Maria, and the "Credo" or Apostles' Creed, all in the same dialect; and I here give the last of these, as being not difficult to follow:

Ich leve ine God, Vader almighti, makere of hevene and of erthe. And ine Iesu Crist, His zone onlepi [*only son*], oure lhord, thet y-kend [*conceived*] is of the Holy Gost, y-bore of Marie mayde, y-pyned [*was crucified*, lit. *made to suffer*] onder Pouns Pilate, y-nayled a rode [*on a cross*], dyad, and be-bered; yede [*went*] doun to helle; thane thridde day aros vram the dyade; steay [*rose, ascended*] to hevenes; zit [*sitteth*] athe [*on the*] right half of God the Vader almighti; thannes to comene He is, to deme the quike and the dyade. Ich y-leve ine the Holy Gost; holy cherche generalliche; Mennesse of halyen [*communion of holy-ones*]; Lesnesse of zennes [*remission of sins*]; of vlesse [*flesh, body*] arizinge; and lyf evrelestinde. Zuo by hyt [*so be it*].

A few remarks may well be made here on some of the peculiarities of Southern English that appear here. The use of *v* for *f* (as in *vader, vram, vlesshe*), and of *z* for *s* (as in *zone, zit, zennes*) are common to this day, especially in Somersetshire. The spelling *lhord* reminds us that many Anglo-Saxon words began with *hl*, one of them being *hlāfweard*, later *hlāford*, a lord; and this *hl* is a symbol denoting the so-called "whispered *l*," sounded much as if an aspirate were prefixed to the *l*, and still common in Welsh, where it is denoted by *ll*, as in *llyn*, a lake. In every case, modern English substitutes for it the ordinary *l*, though *lh* (= *hl*) was in use in 1340 in Southern. The prefix *y-*, representing the extremely common A.S. (Anglo-Saxon) prefix *ge-*, was kept up in Southern much longer than in the other dialects, but has now disappeared; the form *y-clept* being archaic. The plural suffix *-en*, as in *haly-en*, holy ones, saints, is due to the fact that Southern admitted the use of that suffix very freely, as in *cherch-en*, churches, *sterr-en*, stars, etc.; whilst Northern only admitted five such plurals, viz. *egh-en*, *ey-en*, eyes (Shakespeare's *eyne*), *hos-en*, stockings, *ox-en*, *shoo-n*, shoes, and *fā-n*, foes; *ox-en* being the sole survivor, since *shoon* (as in *Hamlet*, IV iv 26) is archaic. The modern *child-r-en*, *breth-r-en*, are really double plurals; Northern employed the more original forms *childer* and *brether*, both of which, and especially the former, are still in dialectal use. *Evrelest-inde* exhibits the Southern *-inde* for present participles.

But the word *zennes*, sins, exhibits a peculiarity that is almost solely Kentish, and seldom found elsewhere, viz. the use of *e* for *i*. The explanation of this rests on an elementary lesson in Old English phonology, which it will do the reader no harm to acquire. The modern symbol *i* (when denoting the *short* sound, as in *pit*) really does double duty. It sometimes represents the A.S. short *i*, as in *it* (A.S. *hit*), *sit* (A.S. *sittan*), *bitten* (A.S. *bĭten*), etc.; and sometimes the A.S. short *y*, as in *pyt*, a pit. The sound of the A.S. short *i* was much the same as in modern English; but that of the short *y* was different, as it denoted the "mutated" form of short *u* for which German has a special symbol, viz. *ü*, the sound intended being that of the German *ü* in *schützen*, to protect. In the latter case, Kentish usually has the vowel *e*, as in the modern Kentish *pet*, a pit, and in the surname *Petman* (at Margate), which means *pitman*; and as the A.S. for "sin" was *synn* (dat. *synne*), the Kentish form was *zenne*, since Middle English substantives often represent the A.S. dative case. The Kentish plural had the double form, *zennes* and *zennen*, both of which occur in the *Ayenbite*, as might have been expected.

The poet Gower, who completed what may be called the first edition of his poem named the *Confessio Amantis* (or Confession of a Lover) in 1390, was a Kentish man, and well acquainted with the Kentish dialect. He took advantage of this to introduce, occasionally, Kentish forms into his verse; apparently for the sake of securing a rime more easily. See this discussed at p. ci of vol. II of Macaulay's edition of Gower. I may illustrate this by noting that in *Conf. Amant.* i 1908, we find *pitt* riming with *witt,* whereas in the same, v 4945, *pet* rimes with *let.*

We know that, in 1386, the poet Chaucer was elected a knight of the shire for Kent, and in 1392–3 he was residing at Greenwich. He evidently knew something of the Kentish dialect; and he took advantage of the circumstance, precisely as Gower did, for varying his rimes. The earliest example of this is in his *Book of the Duchess,* l. 438, where he uses the Kentish *ken* instead of *kin* (A.S. *cynn*) in order to secure a rime for *ten.* In the *Canterbury Tales,* E 1057, he has *kesse,* to kiss (A.S. *cyssan*), to rime with *stedfastnesse.* In the same, A 1318, he has *fulfille,* to fulfil (cf. A.S. *fyllan,* to fill), to rime with *wille*; but in Troilus, iii 510, he changes it to *fulfelle,* to rime with *telle*; with several other instances of a like kind.

It is further remarkable that some Kentish forms seem to have established themselves in standard English, as when we use *dent* with the sense of *dint* (A.S. *dynt*). When we speak of *the left hand,* the form *left* is really Kentish, and occurs in the *Ayenbite of Inwyt*; the Midland form is properly *lift,* which is common enough in Middle English; see the *New English Dictionary,* s.v. *Left,* adj. *Hemlock* is certainly a Kentish form; cf. A.S. *hymlice,* and see the *New English Dictionary.* So also is *kernel* (A.S. *cyrnel*);

knell (A.S. *cnyllan*, verb); *merry* (A.S. *myrge, myrige*); and perhaps *stern*, adj. (A.S. *styrne*).

There are some excellent remarks upon the vocalism of the Kentish dialect in Middle English by W. Heuser, in the German periodical entitled *Anglia*, vol. XVII pp. 73—90.

CHAPTER VIII

THE MERCIAN DIALECT

I. East Midland

The Mercian district lies between the Northern and Southern, occupying an irregular area which it is very difficult to define. On the east coast it reached from the mouth of the Humber to that of the Thames. On the western side it seems to have included a part of Lancashire, and extended from the mouth of the Lune to the Bristol Channel, exclusive of a great part of Wales.

There were two chief varieties of it which differed in many particulars, viz. the East Midland and the West Midland. The East Midland included, roughly speaking, the counties of Lincoln, Rutland, Northampton, and Buckingham, and all the counties (between the Thames and Humber) to the east of these, viz. Cambridge, Huntingdon, Bedford, Hertford, Middlesex, Norfolk, Suffolk, and Essex. We must also certainly include, if not Oxfordshire, at any rate the city of Oxford. This is by far the most important group of counties, as it was the East Midland that finally prevailed over the rest, and was at last accepted as a standard, thus rising from the position of a dialect to be the language of the Empire. The Midland prevailed over the Northern and Southern dialects because it was intermediate between them, and so helped to interpret between North and South; and the East Midland prevailed over the Western because it contained within its area all three of the chief literary centres, namely, Oxford, Cambridge, and London. It follows from this that the Old Mercian dialect is of greater interest than either the Northumbrian or the Anglo-Saxon.

Unfortunately, the amount of extant Old Mercian, before the Conquest, is not very large, and it is only of late years that the MSS. containing it have been rightly understood. Practically, the study of it dates only from 1885, when Dr Sweet published his *Oldest English Texts.*

But there is more Mercian to be found than was at first suspected; and it is desirable to consider this question.

An important discovery was that the language of the oldest Glossaries seems to be Mercian. We have extant no less than four Glossaries in MSS. of as early a date as the eighth century, named respectively, the Epinal, Erfurt, Corpus, and Leyden Glossaries. The first is now at Epinal, in France (in the department Vosges); the second, at Erfurt, near Weimar, in Germany; the third, in Corpus Christi College, Cambridge; and the fourth, at Leyden, in Holland. The Corpus MS. may be taken as typical of the rest. It contains an enumeration of a large number of difficult words, arranged, but imperfectly, in alphabetical order; and after each of these is written its gloss or interpretation. Thus the fifth folio begins as follows:

Abminiculum . adiutorium.	Absida . sacrarium.
Abelena . haeselhnutu.	Abies . etspe.
Abiecit . proiecit.	Ab ineunte ætate . infantia.

The chief interest of these Glossaries lies in the fact that a small proportion of the hard words is explained, not in Latin, but in Mercian English, of which there are two examples in the six glosses here quoted. Thus Abelena, which is another spelling of Abellana or Avellana, "a filbert," is explained as "haeselhnutu"; which is a perfectly familiar word when reduced to its modern form of "hazel-nut." And again, Abies, which usually means "a fir-tree," is here glossed by "etspe." But this is certainly a false spelling, as we see by comparing it with the following glosses in Epinal and Erfurt (Nos. 37, 1006):—"Abies. saeppae—sæpae"; and "Tremulus. aespae—espæ." This shows that the scribe ought to have explained Abies by "saeppae," meaning the tree full of sap, called in French *sapin*; but he confused it with another tree, the "trembling" tree, of which the Old Mercian name was "espe" or "espæ," or "aespae," and he miswrote *espe* as *etspe*, inserting a needless *t*. This last tree is the one which Chaucer called the *asp* in l. 180 of his *Parliament of Fowls*, but in modern times the adjectival suffix *-en* (as in *gold-en*, *wood-en*) has been tacked on to it, and it is now the *aspen*.

The interpretation of these ancient glosses requires very great care, but they afford a considerable number of interesting results, and are therefore valuable, especially as they give us spellings of the eighth century, which are very scarce.

One of the oldest specimens of Old Mercian that affords intelligible sentences is known as the "Lorica Prayer," because it occurs in the same MS. (Ll. 1. 10 in the Cambridge University Library) as the "Lorica Glosses," or the glosses which accompany a long Latin prayer, really a charm, called "lorica" or "breastplate," because it was recited thrice a day to protect the person who used it from all possible injury and accident. I give this Prayer as illustrating the state of our language about A.D. 850.

And the georne gebide gece and miltse fore alra his haligra gewyrhtum and ge-earningum and boenum be [hiwe]num, tha the *domino deo* gelicedon from fruman middan-geardes; thonne gehereth he thec thorh hiora thingunge. Do thonne fiorthan sithe thin hleor thriga to iorthan, fore alle Godes cirican, and sing thas fers: *domini est salus, saluum fac populum tuum, domine, praetende misericordiam tuam.* Sing thonne *pater noster*.

Gebide thonne fore alle geleaffulle menn *in mundo.* Thonne bistu thone deg dael-niomende thorh Dryhtnes gefe alra theara goda the ænig monn for his noman gedoeth, and thec alle sothfestæ fore thingiath *in caelo et in terra. Amen.*[1]

That is :—

And earnestly pray for-thyself for help and mercy by-reason-of the deeds and merits and prayers of all his saints on-behalf-of the [households] that have pleased the Lord God from the beginning of the world; then will He hear thee because-of their intercession. Bow-down then, at the fourth time, thy face thrice to the earth before all God's church, and sing these verses: The Lord is my salvation, save Thy people, O Lord: show forth Thy mercy. Sing then a pater-noster. Pray then for all believing men in the world. Then shalt thou be, on that day, a partaker, by God's grace, of all the good things that any man doth for His name, and all true-men will intercede for thee in heaven and in earth. Amen.

Another discovery was the assignment of a correct description to the glosses found in a document known as the *Vespasian Psalter*; so called because it is an early Latin Psalter, or book of Psalms, contained in a Cotton MS. in the British Museum, marked with the class-mark "Vespasian, A. 1." This Psalter is accompanied throughout with glosses which were at first mistakenly thought to be in a Northumbrian dialect, and were published as such by the Surtees Society in 1843. They were next, in 1875, wrongly supposed to be Kentish; but since they were printed by Sweet in 1885 it has been shown that they are really

[1] I write *hiwenum* in l. 2 in place of an illegible word.

Mercian. This set of glosses is very important for the study of Old Mercian, because they are rather extensive; they occupy 213 pages of the *Oldest English Texts,* and are followed by 20 more pages of similar glosses to certain Latin canticles and hymns that occur in the same MS.

There are also a few Charters extant in the Mercian dialect, but the earliest contain little else than old forms of the names of persons and places. There are, however, some later Charters, from 836 to 1058 in the Mercian dialect, which contain some boundaries of lands and afford other information. Most of these relate to Worcestershire.

But the most interesting Mercian glosses are those to be found in the Rushworth MS., which has already been mentioned as containing Northumbrian glosses of the Latin Gospels of St Mark, St Luke, and St John. For the Gospel of St Matthew was glossed by the scribe Farman, who was a priest of Harewood, situate on the river Wharfe, in the West Riding of Yorkshire; whose language, accordingly, was Mercian. In my *Principles of English Etymology, First Series* (second edition, 1892), p. 44, I gave a list of words selected from these glosses, in order to show how much nearer they stand, as a rule, to modern English than do the corresponding Anglo-Saxon forms. I here repeat this list, as it is very instructive. The references, such as "5. 15," are to the chapters and verses of St Matthew's Gospel, as printed in my edition of *The Holy Gospels, in Anglo-Saxon, Northumbrian, and Old Mercian Versions, synoptically arranged* (Cambridge, 1871–87). The first column below gives the Modern English form, the second the Old Mercian form (with references), and the third the Anglo-Saxon or Wessex form:

Modern	Old Mercian	Wessex (A.S.)
all	all, 5. 15	eall
are	arun, 19. 28	(*not used*)
betwixt	betwix, 27. 56	betweox
cheek	cēke, 5. 39	cēace
cold	cald, 10. 42	ceald
eke	ēk, 5. 39	ēac
eleven	enlefan, 28. 16	endlufon
eye	ēge, 5. 29	ēage
falleth	falleth, 10. 29	fealleth
fell, *pt. t. pl.*	fellun, 7. 25	fēollon
-fold (*in* ten-fold)	-fald, 19. 29	-feald
gall, *sb.*	galla, 27. 34	gealla
half, *sb.*	half, 20. 23	healf
halt, *adj.*	halt, 11. 5	healt
heard, *pt. t. s.*	(ge)hērde, 2. 3	(ge)hīerde
lie (*tell lies*)	līgan, 5. 11	lēogan
light, *sb.*	līht, 5. 16	lēoht
light, *adj.*	liht, 11. 30	leoht
narrow	naru, 7. 14	nearu
old	áld, 9. 16	eald
sheep	scēp, 25. 32	scēap
shoes	scōas, 10. 10	scēos, scȳ
silver	sylfur, 10. 9	seolfor
slept, *pt. t. pl.*	sleptun, 13. 25	slēpon

	Modern	Old Mercian	Wessex (A.S.)
25	sold, *pp.*	sald, 10. 19	seald
	spit, *vb.*	spittan, 27. 30	spǣtan
	wall	wall, 21. 33	weall
	yard (*rod*)	ierd, 10. 10	gyrd
	yare (*ready*)	iara, 22. 4	gearo
30	yoke	ioc, 11. 29	geoc
	youth	iuguth, 19. 20	geoguth

In l. 5, the scribe Farman miswrote *caldas* as *galdas*, in Matt. x 42; but it is a mere mistake. In l. 20, the accent over the *a* in *áld* is marked in the MS., though the vowel was not originally long.

Even a glance at this comparative table reveals a peculiarity of the Wessex dialect which properly belongs neither to Mercian nor to Modern English, viz. the use of the diphthong *ea* (in which each vowel was pronounced separately) instead of simple *a*, before the sounds denoted by *l*, *r*, *h*, especially when another consonant follows. We find accordingly such Wessex forms as *eall, ceald, fealleth, -feald, gealla, healf, healt, nearu, eald, seald, weall, gearo*, where the Old Mercian has simply *all, cald, falleth, -fald, galla, half, halt, naru, ald, sald, wall, iara.* Similarly, Wessex has the diphthongs *ēa, ēo*, in which the former element is long, where the Old Mercian has simply *ē* or *ī*. We find accordingly the Wessex *cēace, ēac, ēage, scēap*, as against the Mercian *cēke, ēk, ēge, scēp*; and the Wessex *lēogan, lēoht*, as against the Mercian *līgan, līht.*

I have now mentioned nearly all the examples of Old Mercian to be found before the Conquest. After that event it was still the Southern dialect that prevailed, and there is scarcely any Mercian (or Midland) to be found except in the Laud MS. of the *Anglo-Saxon Chronicle*, which was written at Peterborough. See the extract, describing the miserable state of England during the reign of Stephen, in *Specimens of Early English*, Part I.

It was about the year 1200 that the remarkable work appeared that is known by the name of *The Ormulum*, written in the North-East Midland of Lincolnshire, which is the first clear example of the form which our literary language was destined to assume. It is an extremely long and dreary poem of about 10,000 long lines, written in a sadly monotonous unrimed metre; and it contains an introduction, paraphrases relating to the gospels read in the church during the year, and homilies upon the same. It was named *Ormulum* by the author after his own name, which was Orm; and the sole existing MS. is probably in the handwriting of Orm himself, who employed a phonetic spelling of his own invention which he strongly recommends. Owing to this circumstance and to the fact that his very regular metre leaves no doubt as to his grammatical forms, this otherwise uninviting poem has a high philological value. In my book entitled *The Chaucer Canon*, published at

Oxford in 1900, I quote 78 long lines from the *Ormulum*, reduced to a simpler system of spelling, at pp. 9—14; and, at pp. 15—18, I give an analysis of the suffixes employed by Orm to mark grammatical inflexions. At pp. 30—41, I give an analysis of similar inflexions as employed by Chaucer, who likewise employed the East Midland dialect, but with such slight modifications of Orm's language as were due to his living in London instead of Lincolnshire, and to the fact that he wrote more than 150 years later. The agreement, as to grammatical usages, of these two authors is extremely close, allowing for lapse of time; and the comparison between them gives most indubitable and valuable results. There is no better way of learning Chaucer's grammar.

As East Midland was spread over a wide area, there are, as might be expected, some varieties of it. The dialects of Lincolnshire and of Norfolk were not quite the same, and both differed somewhat from that of Essex and Middlesex; but the general characteristics of all three sub-dialects are very much alike. As time went on, the speech of the students of Oxford and Cambridge was closely assimilated to that of the court as held in London; and this "educated" type was naturally that to which Caxton and the great writers of the sixteenth century endeavoured to conform.

We have one ancient specimen of the London

dialect which is eminently authentic and valuable, and has the additional advantage of being exactly dated. This is the document known as "The only English Proclamation of Henry III," issued on Oct. 18, 1258. Its intention was to confirm to the people the "Provisions of Oxford," a charter of rights that had been wrested from the king, from which we may conclude that the Proclamation was issued by Henry rather by compulsion than by his own free will. There is a note at the end which tells us that a copy was sent to every shire in England and to Ireland. If every copy had been preserved, we should have a plentiful supply. As it is, only two copies have survived. One is the copy which found its way to Oxford; and the other is the original from which the copies were made, which has been carefully preserved for six centuries and a half in the Public Record Office in London[1]. I here give the contents of the original, substituting *y* (at the beginning of a word) or *gh* (elsewhere) for the symbol ȝ, and *th* for the symbol þ, and *v* for *u* when between two vowels.

¶ Henri, thurgh Godes fultume king on Engleneloande, Lhoaverd on Yrloande, Duk on Norm(andi), on Aquitaine, and Eorl on Aniow, send igretinge to alle hise holde ilærde and ileawede on Huntendoneschire: thæt witen ye wel alle, thæt we willen and unnen thæt, thæt ure rædesmen alle, other the moare dæl of heom, thæt beoth ichosen thurgh us and thurgh thæt loandes

[1] See facsimile at end of this volume.

folk on ure kuneriche, habbeth idon and schullen don in the worthnesse of Gode and on ure treowthe, for the freme of the loande, thurgh the besighte of than to-foren iseide redesmen, beo stedefæst and ilestinde in alle thinge, abuten ænde.

And we hoaten alle ure treowe, in the treowthe thæt heo us ogen, thæt heo stedefæstliche healden, and swerien to healden and to werien, tho isetnesses thæt beon imakede and beon to makien, thurgh than to-foren iseide rædesmen, other thurgh the moare dæl of hem, alswo alse hit is biforen iseid; And thæt æhc other helpe thæt for to done bi than ilche othe, ayenes alle men, right for to done and to foangen. And noan ne nime of loande ne of eghte, wherthurgh this besighte mughe beon ilet other iwersed on onie wise.

And yif oni other onie cumen her onyenes, we willen and hoaten thæt alle ure treowe heom healden deadliche ifoan. And for thæt we willen thæt this beo stedefæst and lestinde, we senden yew this writ open, iseined with ure seel, to halden a-manges yew ine hord.

Witnesse us selven æt Lundene, thane eghtetenthe day on the monthe of Octobre, in the two and fowertighthe yeare of ure cruninge.

And this wes idon ætforen ure isworene redesmen, Boneface archebischop on Kanterburi, Walter of Cantelow, bischop on Wirechestre, Simon of Muntfort, eorl on Leirchestre, Richard of Clare, eorl on Glowchestre and on Hurtforde, Roger Bigod, eorl on Northfolke and marescal on Engleneloande, Perres of Sauveye, Willelm of Fort, eorl on Aubemarle, Iohan of Pleisseiz, eorl on Warewike, Iohan Geffreës sune, Perres of Muntfort, Richard of Grey, Roger of Mortemer, James of Aldithel; and ætforen othre inoghe.

¶ And al on tho ilche worden is isend in-to ævrihce othre shcire over al thære kuneriche on Engleneloande, and ek in-tel Irelonde.

This document presents at first sight many unfamiliar forms, but really differs from Modern English mainly in the spelling, which of course represents the pronunciation of that period. The grammar is perfectly intelligible, and this is the surest mark of similarity of language; we may, however, note the use of *send* as a contraction of *sendeth*, and of *oni* for "any man" in the singular, while *onie*, being plural, represents "any men."

The other chief variations are in the vocabulary or word-list, due to the fact that this Proclamation is older than the reigns of the first three Edwards, which was the period when so many words of Anglo-Norman origin entered our language, displacing many words of native origin that thus became obsolete; though some were exchanged for other *native* words. We may notice, for example, *fultume*, "assistance"; *holde*, "faithful"; *ilærde and ileawede*, "learned and unlearned"; *unnen*, "grant"; *rædesmen*, "councillors"; *kuneriche*, "kingdom"; and so on. I subjoin a closely literal translation, retaining awkward expressions.

¶ Henry, through God's assistance, king in England, Lord in Ireland, Duke in Normandy, in Aquitaine, and Earl in Anjou, sendeth greeting to all his faithful, learned and unlearned, in Huntingdonshire; that wit ye well all, that we will and grant that which our councillors all, or the more deal (*part*) of them, that be chosen through us and through the land's folk in our kingdom, have done and shall do in the worship of God and in our truth, for the benefit of the land, through the provision of the beforesaid councillors, be steadfast and lasting in all things without end. And we command all our true-men, in the truth that they us owe, that they steadfastly hold, and swear to hold and to defend, the statutes that be made and be to make, through the aforesaid councillors, or through the more deal of them, even as it is before said; and that each help other that for to do, by the same oath, against all men, right for to do and to receive. And (let) none take of land nor of property, wherethrough this provision may be let or worsened in any wise. And if any-man or any-men come here-against, we will and command that all our true-men hold them (as) deadly foes. And for that we will that this be steadfast and lasting, we send you this writ open, signed with our seal, to hold amongst you in hoard. Witness us-selves at London, the eighteenth day in the month of October, in the two and fortieth year of our crowning. And this was done before our sworen councillors, Boneface, archbishop of Canterbury, Walter of Cantelow, bishop of Worcester, Simon of Muntfort, earl of Leicester,...and before others enough.

¶ And all in the same words is sent into every other shire over all the kingdom in England, and eke into Ireland.

In the year 1303, Robert Manning, of Bourn in Lincolnshire, translated a French poem entitled *Manuel des Pechiez* (Manual of Sins) into very fair East Midland verse, giving to his translation the title of *Handlyng Synne.* Many of the verses are easy and smooth, and the poem clearly shows us that the East Midland dialect was by this time at least the equal of the others, and that the language was good enough to be largely permanent. When we read such lines as:

Than seyd echone that sate and stode,
Here comth Pers, that never dyd gode—

we have merely to modernise the spelling, and we at once have:

> Then said each one that sat and stood,
> Here cometh Pierce, that never did good.

These are lines that could be written now.

An extract from Manning's *Handlyng Synne* is given in *Specimens of Early English*, Part II, most of which can be read with ease. The obsolete words are not very numerous, and we meet now and then with half a dozen consecutive lines that would puzzle no one.

It is needless to pursue the history of this dialect further. It had, by this time, become almost the standard language, differing from Modern English chiefly in date, and consequently in pronunciation. We pass on from Manning to Chaucer, from Chaucer to Lydgate and Caxton, and from Caxton to Lord Surrey and Sackville and Spenser, without any real change in the actual dialect employed, but only in the form of it.

II. West Midland

We have seen that there are two divisions of the Mercian dialect, into East and West Midland.

The West Midland does not greatly differ from the East Midland, but it approaches more nearly, in some respects, to the Northumbrian. The greatest distinction seems to be in the present and past participles of verbs. In the West Midland, the present participle frequently ends in *-and*, as in Northumbrian, especially in the Northern part of the Midland area. The East Midland usually employs *-ende* or *-inge* instead. In the West Midland, the prefix *i-* or *y-* is seldom used for the past participle, whilst the East Midland admits it more freely. In the third person singular of the present tense, the West Midland favours the Northern suffix *-es* or *-is*; whilst the East Midland favours the Southern suffix *-eth*. The suffix *-us* appears to be altogether peculiar to West Midland, in which it occurs occasionally; and the same is true of *-ud* for *-ed* in the preterite of a weak verb.

There is a rather early West Midland *Prose Psalter*, belonging to the former half of the fourteenth century, which was edited for the Early English Text Society by Dr Karl Bülbring in 1891.

The curious poem called *William of Palerne* (Palermo) or *William and the Werwolf*, written in alliterative verse about 1350–60, and edited by me for the E.E.T.S. in 1867, seems to be in a form of West Midland, and has been claimed for Shropshire; nothing is known as to its author.

The very remarkable poem called *The Pearl*, and three *Alliterative Poems* by the same author, were first edited by Dr Morris for the E.E.T.S. in 1864; with a preface in which the peculiarities of the dialect were discussed. Dr Morris showed that the grammatical forms are uniform and consistent throughout, and may be safely characterised as being West Midland. Moreover, they are frequently very like Northumbrian, and must belong to the Northern area of the West Midland dialect. "Much," says Dr Morris, "may be said in favour of their Lancashire origin."

The MS. which contains the above poems also contains the excellent alliterative romance-poem named *Sir Gawayne and the Green Knight*, evidently written by the same author; so that this poem also may be considered as a specimen of West Midland. For further particulars, see the "Grammatical Details" given in Dr Morris's preface to *The Pearl*, etc., pp. xxviii–xl. *Sir Gawayne* was likewise edited by Morris in 1864.

It would not be easy to trace the history of this dialect at a later date, and the task is hardly necessary. It was soon superseded in literary use by the East Midland, with which it had much in common.

CHAPTER IX

FOREIGN ELEMENTS IN THE DIALECTS

THERE is a widely prevalent notion that the speakers of English Dialects employ none but native words; and it is not uncommon for writers who have more regard for picturesque effect than for accuracy to enlarge upon this theme, and to praise the dialects at the expense of the literary language. Of course there is a certain amount of truth in this, but it would be better to look into the matter a little more closely.

A very little reflection will show that dialect-speakers have always been in contact with some at least of those who employ words that belong rather, or once belonged, to foreign nations. Even shop-keepers are familiar with such words as *beef*, *mutton*, *broccoli*, *soda*, *cork*, *sherry*, *brandy*, *tea*, *coffee*, *sugar*, *sago*, and many more such words that are now quite familiar to every one. Yet *beef* and *mutton* are Norman; *broccoli* and *soda* are Italian; *cork* and *sherry* are Spanish; *brandy* is Dutch; *tea* is Chinese; *coffee* is Arabic; *sugar* is of Sanskrit origin; and *sago* is Malay. It must be evident that many similar words, having reference to very various useful things, have long ago drifted into the dialects from the literary language. Hence the purity of the dialects from contamination with foreign influences is merely comparative, not absolute.

Our modern language abounds with words borrowed from many foreign tongues; but a large number of them have come to us since 1500. Before that date the chief languages from which it was possible for us to borrow words were British or Gaelic, Irish, Latin, Greek (invariably through the medium of Latin), Hebrew (in a small degree, through the medium of Latin), Arabic (very slightly, and indirectly), Scandinavian, and French. A few words as to most of these are sufficient.

It is not long since a great parade was made of our borrowings from "Celtic"; it was very easy to give a wild guess that an obscure word was "Celtic"; and the hardihood of the guesser was often made to take the place of evidence. The fact is that there is no such language as "Celtic"; it is the name of a group of languages, including "British" or Welsh, Cornish, Breton, Manx, Gaelic, and Irish; and it is now incumbent on the etymologist to cite the exact forms in one or more of these on which he relies, so as to adduce some semblance of proof. The result has been an extraordinary shrinkage in the number of alleged Celtic words. The number, in fact, is extremely small, except in special cases. Thus we may expect to find a few Welsh words in the dialects of Cheshire, Shropshire, or Herefordshire, on the Welsh border; and a certain proportion of Gaelic words in Lowland Scotch; though we have no reliable lists of these, and it is remarkable that such words have usually been borrowed at no very early date, and sometimes quite recently. The legacy of words bequeathed to us by the ancient Britons is surprisingly small; indeed, it is very difficult to point to many clear cases. The question is considered in my *Principles of English Etymology, Series I*, pp. 443–452, to which I may refer the reader; and a list of words of (probably) Celtic origin is given in my larger *Etymological Dictionary*, ed. 1910, p. 765. It is also explained, in my *Primer of English Etymology*, that, in the fifth century, the time of Hengist's invasion, "the common language of the more educated classes among the British was Latin, which was in use as a literary language and as the language of the British Christian Church. Hence, the Low German tribes [of invaders] found no great necessity for learning ancient British; and this explains the fact, which would otherwise be extraordinary, that modern English contains but a very small Celtic element." Of the Celts that remained within the English pale, it is certain that, in a very short time, they accepted the necessity of learning Anglian or Saxon, and lost their previous language altogether. Hence, in many dialects, as for example, in the East Midland district, the amount of words of "British" origin is practically *nil*. For further remarks on this subject, see Chapter v of *Anglo-Saxon Britain*, by Grant Allen, London, n.d.

I here give a tentative list of some Celtic words found in dialects. Their etymologies are discussed in my *Etymological Dictionary* (1910), as they are also found in literary use; and the words are fully explained in the *English Dialect Dictionary*, which gives all their senses, and enumerates the counties in which they are found. It is doubtless imperfect, as I give only words that are mostly well known, and can be found, indeed, in the *New English Dictionary*. I give only one sense of each, and mark it as N., M., or S. (Northern, Midland, or Southern), as the case may be. The symbol "gen." means "in general use"; and "Sc." means Lowland Scotch.

Art, or *airt*, Sc., a direction of the wind; *banshee*, Irish, a female spirit who warns families of a death; *beltane*, N., the first of May; *bin*, M., a receptacle; *boggart*, *bogle*, N., M., a hobgoblin; *bragget*, N., M., a drink made of honey and ale; *brat*, N., M., a cloth, clout; *brock*, gen., a badger; *bug*, N., a bogy; *bugaboo*, N., M., a hobgoblin; *capercailyie*, Sc., a bird; *cateran*, Sc., a Highland robber; *char*, N., a fish; *clachan*, Sc., a hamlet; *clan*, N., M., a class, set of people; *claymore*, Sc., a two-handed sword; *colleen*, Irish, a young girl; *combe*, gen., the head of a valley; *coracle*, M., a wicker boat; *coronach*, Sc., a dirge; *corrie*, Sc., a circular hollow in a hill-side; *cosher*, Irish, a feast; *crag*, *craig*, N., a rock; *crowd*, N., S., a fiddle; *dulse*, N., an edible sea-weed; *dun*, gen., brown, greyish; *duniwassal*, Sc., a gentleman of secondary rank; *fillibeg*, Sc., a short kilt; *flummery*, Sc., M., oatmeal boiled in water; *gallowglass*, Sc., Irish, an armed foot-soldier; *galore*, gen., in abundance; *gillie*, Sc., a man-servant; *gull*, a name of various birds; *hubbub*, *hubbaboo*, Irish, a confused clamour; *inch*, Sc., Irish, a small island; *ingle*, N., M., fire, fire-place; *kelpie*, Sc., a water-spirit; *kibe*, gen., a chilblain; *linn*, N., a pool; *loch*, N., *lough*, Irish, a lake; *metheglin*, M., S., beer made from honey; *omadhaun*, Irish, a simpleton; *pose*, gen. (but perhaps obsolete), a catarrh; *rapparee*, Sc., Irish, a vagabond; *shillelagh*, Irish, a cudgel; *skain*, *skean*, Sc., Irish, a knife, dagger; *sowens*, *sowans*, Sc., a dish made from oatmeal-husks steeped in water (from Gael. *sùghan*, the juice of sowens); *spalpeen*, Irish, a rascal; *spleuchan*, Sc., Irish, a pouch, a purse; *strath*, N., a valley; *strathspey*, Sc., a dance, named from the valley of the river Spey; *tocher*, N., a dowry; *usquebaugh*, Sc., Irish, whiskey; *wheal*, Cornish, a mine.

Latin is a language from which English has

borrowed words in every century since the year 600. In my *Principles of English Etymology, First Series*, Chap. XXI, I give a list of Latin words imported into English before the Norman Conquest. Several of these must be familiar in our dialects; we can hardly suppose that country people do not know the meaning of ark, beet, box, candle, chalk, cheese, cook, coulter, cup, fennel, fever, font, fork, inch, kettle, kiln, kitchen, and the like. Indeed, *ark* is quite a favourite word in the North for a large wooden chest, used for many purposes; and Kersey explains it as "a country word for a large chest to put fruit or corn in." *Candle* is so common that it is frequently reduced to *cannel*; and it has given its name to "cannel coal." Every countryman is expected to be able to distinguish "between chalk and cheese." *Coulter* appears in ten dialect forms, and one of the most familiar agricultural implements is a pitch-*fork*. The influence of Latin requires no further illustration.

I also give a list of early words of Greek origin; some of which are likewise in familiar use. I may instance alms, angel, bishop, butter, capon, chest, church, clerk, copper, devil, dish, hemp, imp, martyr, paper (ultimately of Egyptian origin), plaster, plum, priest, rose, sack, school, silk, treacle, trout. Of course the poor old woman who says she is "a martyr to toothache" is quite unconscious that she is talking Greek. Probably she is not without some smattering of

Persian, and knows the sense of lilac, myrtle, orange, peach, and rice; of Sanskrit, whence pepper and sugar-candy; of Arabic, whence coffee, cotton, jar, mattress, senna, and sofa; and she will know enough Hebrew, partly from her Bible, to be quite familiar with a large number of biblical names, such as Adam and Abraham and Isaac, and very many more, not forgetting the very common John, Joseph, Matthew, and Thomas, and the still more familiar Jack and Jockey; and even with a few words of Hebrew origin, such as alleluia, balm, bedlam, camel, cider, and sabbath. The discovery of the New World has further familiarised us all with chocolate and tomato, which are Mexican; and with potato, which is probably old Caribbean. These facts have to be borne in mind when it is too rashly laid down that words in English dialects are of English origin.

Foreign words of this kind are, however, not very numerous, and can easily be allowed for. And, as has been said, our vocabulary admits also of a certain amount of Celtic. It remains to consider what other sources have helped to form our dialects. The two most prolific in this respect are Scandinavian and French, which require careful consideration.

It is notorious that the Northern dialect admits Scandinavian words freely; and the same is true, to a lesser degree, of East Midland. They are rare in Southern, and in the Southern part of West Midland.

The constant invasions of the Danes, and the subjection of England under the rule of three Danish kings, Canute and his two successors, have very materially increased our vocabulary; and it is remarkable that they have perhaps done more for our dialects than for the standard language. The ascendancy of Danish rule was in the eleventh century; but (with a few exceptions) it was long before words which must really have been introduced at that time began to appear in our literature. They must certainly have been looked upon, at the first, as being rustic or dialectal. I have nowhere seen it remarked, and I therefore call attention to the fact, that a certain note of rustic origin still clings to many words of this class; and I would instance such as these: bawl, bloated, blunder, bungle, clog, clown, clumsy, to cow, to craze, dowdy, dregs, dump, and many more of a like character. I do not say that such words cannot be employed in serious literature; but they require skilful handling.

For further information, see the chapter on "The Scandinavian Element in English," in my *Principles of English Etymology, Series I.*

With regard to dialectal Scandinavian, see the List of English Words, as compared with Icelandic, in my Appendix to Cleasby and Vigfusson's *Icelandic Dictionary.* In this long list, filling 80 columns, the dialectal words are marked with a dagger (†). But the list of these is by no means exhaustive, and it will require a careful search through the pages of the *English Dialect Dictionary* to do justice to the wealth of this Old Norse element. There is an excellent article on this subject by Arnold Wall, entitled "A Contribution towards the Study of the Scandinavian element in the English Dialects," printed in the German periodical entitled *Anglia, Neue Folge,* Band VIII, 1897.

I now give a list, a mere selection, of some of the more remarkable words of Scandinavian origin that are known to our dialects. For their various uses and localities, see the *English Dialect Dictionary*; and for their etymologies, see my Index to Cleasby and Vigfusson. Many of these words are well approved and forcible, and may perhaps be employed hereafter to reinforce our literary language.

Addle, to earn; *and* (in Barbour, *aynd*), sb., breath; *arder,* a ploughing; *arr,* a scar; *arval,* a funeral repast; *aund,* fated, destined; *bain,* ready, convenient; *bairns' lakings,* children's playthings; *beck,* a stream; *big,* to build; *bigg,* barley; *bing,* a heap; *birr,* impetus; *blaeberry,* a bilberry; *blather, blether,* empty noisy talk; *bouk,* the trunk of the body; *boun,* ready; *braid,* to resemble, to take after; *brandreth,* an iron framework over a fire; *brant,* steep; *bro,* a foot-bridge with a single rail; *bule, bool,* the curved handle of a bucket; *busk,* to prepare oneself, dress; *caller*, fresh, said of fish, etc.; *carle*, a rustic, peasant; *carr*, moist ground; *cleck*, to hatch (as chickens); *cleg*, a horse-fly; *coup*, to exchange, to barter; *dag*, dew; *daggle*, to trail in the wet; *dowf*, dull, heavy, stupid; *dump*, a deep pool.

Elding, *eilding*, fuel; *ettle*, to intend, aim at; *feal*, to hide; *fell*, a hill; *fey*, doomed, fated to die; *flake*, a hurdle; *force*, a water-fall; *gab*, idle talk; *gain*, adj., convenient, suitable; *galt*, a hog; *gar*, to cause, to make; *garn*, yarn; *garth*, a field, a yard; *gate*, a way, street; *ged*, a pike; *gilder*, a snare, a fishing-line; *gilt*, a young sow; *gimmer*, a young ewe; *gloppen*, to scare, terrify; *glore*, to stare, to glow; *goam*, *gaum*, to stare idly, to gape, whence *gomeril*, a blockhead; *gowk*, a cuckoo, a clown; *gowlan*, *gollan*, a marigold; *gowpen*, a double handful; *gradely*, respectable; *graithe*, to prepare; *grice*, a young pig; *haaf*, the open sea; *haver*, oats; *how*, a hillock, mound; *immer-goose*, *ember-goose*, the great Northern diver; *ing*, a lowlying meadow; *intake*, a newly enclosed or reclaimed portion of land; *keld*, a spring of water; *kenning*, knowledge, experience; *kilp*, *kelp*, the iron hook in a chimney on which pots are hung; *kip*, to catch fish in a particular way; *kittle*, to tickle; *lain*, *lane*, to conceal; *lair*, a muddy place, a quicksand; *lait*, to seek; *lake*, to play; *lathe*, a barn; *lax*, a salmon; *lea*, a scythe; *leister*, a fish-spear with prongs and barbs; *lift*, the air, sky; *lig*, to lie down;

lispund, a variable weight; *lit,* to dye; *loon,* the Northern diver; *lowe,* a flame, a blaze.

Mense, respect, reverence, decency, sense; *mickle,* great; *mirk,* dark; *morkin,* a dead sheep; *muck,* dirt; *mug,* fog, mist, whence *muggy,* misty, close, dull; *neif, neive,* the fist; *ouse, ouze,* to empty out liquid, to bale out a boat; *paddock,* a frog, a toad; *quey,* a young heifer; *rae,* a sailyard; *rag,* hoarfrost, rime; *raise,* a cairn, a tumulus; *ram, rammish,* rank, rancid; *rip,* a basket; *risp,* to scratch; *rit,* to scratch slightly, to score; *rawk, roke,* a mist; *roo,* to pluck off the wool of sheep instead of shearing them; *roose,* to praise; *roost, roust,* a strong sea-current, a race.

Sark, a shirt; *scarf,* a cormorant; *scopperil,* a teetotum; *score,* a gangway down to the sea-shore; *screes,* rough stones on a steep mountain-side, really for *screethes* (the *th* being omitted as in *clothes*), from Old Norse *skriða,* a land-slip on a hill-side; *scut,* a rabbit's tail; *seave,* a rush; *sike,* a small rill, gutter; *sile,* a young herring; *skeel,* a wooden pail; *skep,* a basket, a measure; *skift,* to shift, remove, flit; *skrike,* to shriek; *slocken,* to slake, quench; *slop,* a loose outer garment; *snag,* a projecting end, a stump of a tree; *soa,* a large round tub; *spae,* to foretell, to prophesy; *spean,* a teat, (as a verb) to wean; *spelk,* a splinter, thin piece of wood; *steg,* a gander; *storken,* to congeal; *swale,* a shady place; *tang,* the prong of a fork, a tongue of land; *tarn,* a mountain pool;

tath, manure, *tathe*, to manure; *ted*, to spread hay; *theak*, to thatch; *thoft*, a cross-bench in a boat; *thrave*, twenty-four sheaves, or a certain measure of corn; *tit*, a wren; *titling*, a sparrow; *toft*, a homestead, an old enclosure, low hill; *udal*, a particular tenure of land; *ug*, to loathe; *wadmel*, a species of coarse cloth; *wake*, a portion of open water in a frozen lake or stream; *wale*, to choose; *wase*, a wisp or small bundle of hay or straw; *whauve*, to cover over, especially with a dish turned upside down; *wick*, a creek, bay; *wick*, a corner, angle.

Another source of foreign supply to the vocabulary of the dialects is French; a circumstance which seems hitherto to have been almost entirely ignored. The opinion has, I think, been expressed more than once, that dialects are almost, if not altogether, free from French influence. Some, however, have called attention, perhaps too much attention, to the French words found in Lowland Scotch; and it is common to adduce always the same set of examples, such as *ashet*, a dish (F. *assiette*, a trencher, plate: Cotgrave), *gigot*, a leg of mutton, and *petticoat-tails*, certain cakes baked with butter (ingeniously altered from *petits gastels*, old form of *petits gâteaux*), by way of illustration. Indeed, a whole book has been written on this subject; see *A Critical Enquiry into the Scottish Language*, by Francisque-Michel, 4to, Edinburgh, 1882. But the importance of the borrowings, chiefly in Scotland, from Parisian French, has been much exaggerated, as in the work just mentioned; and a far more important source has been ignored, viz. Anglo-French, which I here propose to consider.

By Anglo-French is meant the highly important form of French which is largely peculiar to England, and is of the highest value to the philologist. The earliest forms of it were Norman, but it was afterwards supplemented by words borrowed from other French dialects, such as those of Anjou and Poitou, as well as from the Central French of Paris. It was thus developed in a way of its own, and must always be considered, in preference to Old Continental French, when English etymologies are in question. It is true that it came to an end about 1400, when it ceased to be spoken; but at an earlier date it was alive and vigorous, and coined its own peculiar forms. A very simple example is our word *duty*, which certainly was not borrowed from the Old French *devoir*, but from the Anglo-French *duetee*, a word familiar in Old London, but absolutely unknown to every form of continental French.

The point which I have here to insist upon is that not only does our literary language abound with Anglo-French words, but that they are also common enough in our dialects; a point which, as far as I know, is almost invariably overlooked. Neither have our dialects escaped the influence of the Central

French of Paris, and it would have been strange if they had; for the number of French words in English is really very large. It is not always possible to discriminate between the Old French of France and of England, and I shall here consider both sources together, though the Old Norman words can often be easily discerned by any one who is familiar with the Norman peculiarities. Of such peculiarities I will instance three, by way of example. Thus Anglo-French often employs *ei* or *ey* where Old French (i.e. of the continent) has *oi* or *oy*; and English has retained the old pronunciations of *ch* and *j*. Hence, whilst *convoy* is borrowed from French, *convey* is Anglo-French. *Machine* is French, because the *ch* is pronounced as *sh*; but *chine*, the backbone, is Anglo-French. *Rouge* is French, because of the peculiar pronunciation of the final *ge*; but *rage* is Anglo-French; and *jaundice* is Anglo-French, as it has the old *j*. See Chapters III–VI of my *Principles of English Etymology, Second Series.*

A good example of a dialect word is *gantry* or *gauntree*, a wooden stand for barrels, known in varying forms in many dialects. It is rightly derived, in the *E.D.D.*, from *gantier*, which must have been an A.F. (Anglo-French) form, though now only preserved in the Rouchi dialect, spoken on the borders of France and Belgium, and nearly allied to Norman; in fact, M. Hécart, the author of the *Dictionnaire*

Rouchi-Français, says he had heard the word in Normandy, and he gives a quotation for it from Olivier Basselin, a poet who lived in Normandy at the beginning of the fifteenth century. The Parisian form is *chantier*, which Cotgrave explains as "a Gauntrey...for hogs-heads to stand on." Here is a clear example of a word which is of Norman, or A.F., origin; and there must be many more such of which the A.F. form is lost. There is no greater literary disgrace to England than the fact that there is no reasonable Dictionary in existence of Anglo-French, though it contains hundreds of highly important legal terms. It ought, in fact, to have been compiled before either the *English Dialect Dictionary* or the *New English Dictionary*, both of which have suffered from the lack of it.

It would indeed be tedious to enumerate the vast number of French words in our dialects. Many are literary words used in a peculiar sense, often in one that has otherwise been long obsolete; such as *able*, rich; *access*, an ague-fit; *according*, comparatively; *to act*, to show off, be ridiculous; *afraid*, conj., for fear that; *agreeable*, willing; *aim*, to intend; *aisle*, a central thoroughfare in a shop, etc.; *alley*, the aisle of a church; *allow*, to suppose; *anatomy*, a skeleton; *ancient*, an ensign, flag; *anguish*, inflammation; *annoyance*, damage; *anointed*, notoriously vicious; *apron*, the diaphragm of an animal; *apt*, sure; *arbi-*

trary, impatient of restraint; *archangel*, dead nettle; *argue*, to signify; *arrant*, downright; *auction*, an untidy place, a crowd; *avise* (for *advise*), to inform. It is needless to go through the rest of the alphabet.

Moreover, dialect-speakers are quite capable of devising new forms for themselves. It is sufficient to instance *abundation*, abundance; *ablins*, possibly (made from *able*); *argle*, *argie-bargie*, *argle-bargle*, *argufy*, all varieties of the verb *to argue*; and so on.

The most interesting words are those that have survived from Middle English or from Tudor English times. Examples are *aigre*, sour, tart, which is Shakespeare's *eagre*, *Hamlet*, I, v 69; *ambry*, *aumbry*, a cupboard, spelt *almarie* in *Piers the Plowman*, B XIV 246; *arain*, a spider, spelt *yreyn* in Wyclif's translation of Psalm xc 10, which, after all, is less correct; *arles*, money paid on striking a bargain, a highly interesting word, spelt *erles* in the former half of the thirteenth century; *arris*, the angular edge of a cut block of stone, etc., from the O.F. *areste*, L. *arista*, which has been revived by our Swiss mountain-climbers in the form *arête*; *a-sew*, dry, said of cows that give no milk (cf. F. *essuyer*, to dry); *assoilyie*, to absolve, acquit, and *assith*, to compensate, both used by Sir W. Scott; *astre*, *aistre*, a hearth, a Norman word found in 1292; *aunsel*, a steelyard, of which the etymology is given in the *E.D.D.*; *aunter*, an adventure, from the A.F. *aventure*; *aver*, a beast of burden, horse, used by Burns, from the A.F. *aveir*, property, cattle; *averous*, A.F. *averous*, avaricious, in Wyclif's translation of 1 Cor. vi 10.

Here is ample proof of the survival of Anglo-French in our dialects. Indeed, their chief philological use consists in the great antiquity of many of the terms, which often preserve Old English and Anglo-French forms with much fidelity. The charge often brought against dialect speakers of using "corrupt" forms is only occasionally and exceptionally true. Much worse "corruptions" have been made by antiquaries, in order to suit their false etymologies.

CHAPTER X

LATER HISTORY OF THE DIALECTS

WITH the ascendancy of East Midland, and its acceptance as the chief literary language, the other dialects practically ceased to be recorded, with the exception (noted above) of the Scottish Northumbrian. Of English Northumbrian, the sixteenth century tells us nothing beyond what we can glean from belated copies of Northern ballads or such traces of a Northern (apparently a Lancashire) dialect as appear in Spenser's *Shepherd's Calendar*. Fitzherbert's *Boke of Husbandry* (1534) was reprinted for the E.D.S. in 1882. It was written, not by Sir Anthony Fitzherbert, as I erroneously said in the Preface, but by his brother, John Fitzherbert, as has been subsequently shown. It contains a considerable number of dialectal words. Thomas Tusser (1525—1580), born in Essex, wrote *A Hundreth Good Pointes of Husbandrie* (1557), and *Fiue Hundred Pointes of Good Husbandrie* (1573); see the edition by Payne and Herrtage, E.D.S., 1878. He employs many country words, presumably Essex. The dialect assumed by Edgar in Shakespeare's *King Lear* is not to be taken as being very accurate; he talks somewhat like a Somersetshire peasant, but I suppose his speech to be in a conventional stage dialect, such as we find also in *The London Prodigall*, Act II, Sc. 4, where Olyver, "a Devonshire Clothier," uses similar expressions, viz. *chill* for *Ich will*, I will; and *chy vor thee*, I warn thee.

Towards the end of the seventeenth century, the value of dialectal words as helping to explain our English vocabulary began to be recognised. Particular mention may be made of the *Etymologicon Linguæ Anglicanæ*, by Stephen Skinner, London, 1671; and it should be noted that this is the Dictionary upon which Dr Johnson relied for the etymology of native English words. At the same time, we must not forget to note two Dictionaries of a much earlier date, which are of high value. The former of these is the *Promptorium Parvulorum*, completed in 1440, published by the Camden Society in 1865; which contains a rather large proportion of East Anglian words. The second is the *Catholicon Anglicum*, dated 1483, ed. S. J. Herrtage, E.E.T.S., 1881, which is distinctly Northern (possibly of Yorkshire origin).

We find in Skinner occasional mention of Lincolnshire words, with which he was evidently familiar. Examples are: *boggle-boe*, a spectre; *bratt*, an apron;

buffet-stool, a hassock; *bulkar*, explained by Peacock as "a wooden hutch in a workshop or a ship."

The study of modern English Dialects began with the year 1674, when the celebrated John Ray, Fellow of the Royal Society, botanist, zoologist, and collector of local words and proverbs, issued his *Collection of English Words not generally used*; of which a second edition appeared in 1691. See my reprint of these; E.D.S., 1874. This was the first general collection, and one of the best; and after this date (1674) many dialect words appeared in English Dictionaries, such as those of Elisha Coles (1676, and four subsequent editions); John Kersey (1708, etc.); Nathaniel Bailey (1721, etc.); N. Bailey's *Dictionary*, Part II, a distinct work (1727, etc.). The celebrated *Dictionary* by Dr Johnson, 2 vols., folio, London, 1755, owed much to Bailey. Later, we may notice the *Dictionary* by John Ash, London, 1775; and Todd's edition of Johnson, London, 1818. It is needless to mention later works; see the Complete List of Dictionaries, by H. B. Wheatley, reprinted in the E.D.S. Bibliographical List (1877), pp. 3—11; and the long List of Works which more particularly relate to English Dialects in the same, pp. 11—17. Among the latter may be mentioned *A Provincial Glossary*, by F. Grose, London, 1787, second edition 1790; *Supplement to the same*, by the late S. Pegge, F.S.A., London, 1814; and *Glossary of Archaic and Provincial*

Words, by the late Rev. J. Boucher, ed. Hunter and Stevenson, 1832–3. The last of these was attempted on a large scale, but never got beyond the word *Blade*; so that it was practically a failure. The time for producing a real Dialect Dictionary had not yet come; but the valuable *Etymological Dictionary of the Scottish Language*, by J. Jamieson, published at Edinburgh in 4 vols., 4to, in 1808–25, made an excellent beginning.

The nineteenth century not only accumulated for our use a rather large number of general works on Dialects, but also a considerable quantity of works illustrating them separately. I may instance those on the dialect of Bedfordshire, by T. Batchelor, 1809; of Berkshire, by Job Lousley, 1852; Cheshire, by R. Wilbraham, 1820, 1826; East Anglia, by R. Forby, 1830, and by Nall, 1866; Teesdale, co. Durham, by F. T. Dinsdale, 1849; Herefordshire, by G. C. Lewis, 1839; Lincolnshire, by J. E. Brogden, 1866; Northamptonshire, by Miss A. E. Baker, 2 vols., 1854; the North Country, by J. T. Brockett, 1825, 1846; Somersetshire, by J. Jennings, 1825, 1869; Suffolk, by E. Moor, 1823; Sussex, by W. D. Cooper, 1836, 1853; Wiltshire, by J. Y. Akerman, 1842; the Cleveland dialect (Yorks.), by J. C. Atkinson, 1868; the Craven dialect, by W. Carr, 1824; and many more of the older type that are still of value. We have also two fairly good general dictionaries of dialect words; that by T. Wright, 1857, 1869; and that by J. O. Halliwell, 2 vols., 1847, 11th ed., 1889. See the exhaustive Bibliographical List of all works connected with our dialects in the *E.D.D.*, pp. 1–59, at the end of vol. VI.

In 1869 appeared Part I of Dr A. J. Ellis's great work on *Early English Pronunciation*, with especial reference to Shakespeare and Chaucer; followed by Part II of the same, on the Pronunciation of the thirteenth and previous centuries, of Anglo-Saxon, Icelandic, Old Norse, and Gothic. In 1871 appeared Part III of the same, on the Pronunciation of the fourteenth and sixteenth centuries. Part IV was then planned to include the Pronunciation of the seventeenth, eighteenth, and nineteenth centuries, including the Phonology of the Dialects; and for this purpose it was necessary to gain particulars such as could hardly be accomplished without special research. It was partly with this in view, and partly in order to collect material for a really comprehensive dictionary, that, in 1873, I founded the English Dialect Society, undertaking the duties of Secretary and Director. The Society was brought to an end in 1896, after producing 80 publications and collecting much material. Mr Nodal, of Manchester, was Secretary from 1876 to 1893; and from 1893 to 1896 the headquarters of the Society were in Oxford. Besides this, I raised a fund in 1886 for collecting additional material in manuscript, and thus obtained a considerable quantity, which the Rev. A. Smythe Palmer, D.D., in the course of two years and a half, arranged in fair order. But even in 1889 more was required, and the work was then taken in hand by Dr Joseph Wright, who gives the whole account of the means by which, in 1898, he was enabled to issue Vol. I of the *English Dialect Dictionary*. The sixth and concluding volume of this most valuable work was issued in 1905.

To this I refer the reader for all further information, which is there given in a very complete form. At the beginning is a Preface explaining the history of the book; followed by lists of voluntary readers, of unprinted MS. collections, and of correspondents consulted; whilst Vol. VI, besides a Supplement of 179 pages, gives a Bibliography of Books and MSS. quoted, with a full Index; to which is added the *English Dialect Grammar*.

This *English Dialect Grammar* was also published, in 1905, as a separate work, and contains a full account of the phonology of all the chief dialects, the very variable pronunciation of a large number of leading words being accurately indicated by the use of a special set of symbols; the Table of Vowel-sounds is given at p. 13. The Phonology is followed by an Accidence, which discusses the peculiarities of dialect grammar. Next follows a rather large collection of important words, that are differently pronounced in different counties; for example, more than thirty variations are recorded of the pronunciation of the word *house*. The fulness of the Vocabulary in the Dictionary, and the minuteness of the account of the phonology and accidence in the Grammar, leave nothing to desire. Certainly no other country can give so good an account of its Dialects.

CHAPTER XI

THE MODERN DIALECTS

It has been shown that, in the earliest period, we can distinguish three well-marked dialects besides the Kentish, viz. Northumbrian, Mercian, and Anglo-Saxon; and these, in the Middle English period, are known as Northern, Midland, and Southern. The modern dialects are very numerous, but can be arranged under five divisions, two of which may be called Northern and Southern, as before; whilst the other three arise from a division of the widely spread Midland into subdivisions. These may be called, respectively, West Midland, Mid Midland (or simply Midland), and East Midland; and it has been shown that similar subdivisions appear even in the Middle English period.

This arrangement of the modern dialects under five divisions is that adopted by Prof. Wright, who further simplifies the names by using Western in place of West Midland, and Eastern in place of East

Midland. This gives us, as a final result, five divisions of English dialects, viz. Northern, Western, Midland, Eastern, and Southern; to which we must add the dialects of modern Scotland (originally Northern), and the dialects of Ireland, viz. of Ulster (a kind of Northern), Dublin, and Wexford (a kind of Southern).

No map of dialects is here given in illustration, because it is practically impossible to define their boundaries accurately. Such a map was once given by Dr Ellis, but it is only arbitrary; and Prof. Wright expressly says that, in his work also, the boundaries suggested are inexact; they are only given for convenience, as an approximation to the truth. He agrees with Dr Ellis in most of the particulars.

Many of the counties are divided between two, or even three, dialects; I somewhat simplify matters by omitting to mention some of them, so as to give merely a general idea of the chief dialectal localities. For fuller information, see the *Dialect Grammar*.

I. The dialects of Scotland may be subdivided into nine groups:

1. Shetland and Orkney. 2. Caithness. 3. Nairn, Elgin, Banff, Aberdeen. 4. E. Forfar, Kincardine. 5. W. Forfar, most of Perth, parts of Fife and Stirling. 6. S. Ayr, W. Dumfries, Kirkcudbright, Wigton. 7. S.E. Argyle, N. Ayr, Renfrew, Lanark. 8. Kinross, Clackmannan, Linlithgow, Edinburgh, Haddington, Berwick, Peebles. 9. E. Dumfries, Selkirk, Roxburgh.

II. Ireland.—Ulster, Dublin, Wexford.

III. England and Wales, in five divisions: (*a*) Northern; (*b*) Midland; (*c*) Eastern; (*d*) Western, (*e*) Southern.

(*a*) Three groups: 1. Northumberland, N. Durham. 2. S. Durham; most of Cumberland, Westmoreland, N. Lancashire, hilly parts of W. Riding of Yorkshire. 3. N. and E. Ridings of Yorkshire.

(*b*) Ten groups: 1. Lincolnshire. 2. S.E. Lancashire, N.E. Cheshire, N.W. Derby. 3. S.W. Lancashire, S. of the Ribble. 4. Mid Lancashire, Isle of Man. 5. S. Yorkshire; to the S.W. of the Wharfe. 6. Most of Cheshire, N. Staffordshire. 7. Most of Derby. 8. Nottingham. 9. Flint, Denbigh. 10. E. Shropshire, S. Stafford, most of Warwickshire, S. Derby, Leicestershire.

(*c*) Five groups: 1. Cambridge, Rutland, N.E. Northampton. 2. Most of Essex and Hertford, Huntingdon, Bedford, Mid Northampton. 3. Norfolk and Suffolk. 4. Most of Buckingham. 5. Middlesex, S.E. Buckingham, S. Hertford, S.W. Essex.

N.B. S.W. Northampton is Southern; see (*e*), 4.

(*d*) Two groups: 1. W. and S. Shropshire (W. of Severn). 2. Hereford (except E.), Radnor, E. Brecknock.

(*e*) Ten groups. 1. Parts of Pembroke and Glamorgan. 2. Wiltshire, Dorset, N. and E. Somerset, most of Gloucester, S.W. Devon. 3. Most of Hampshire, Isle of Wight, most of Berkshire, S. Surrey, W. Sussex. 4. N. Gloucester, E. Hereford, Worcester, S. Warwick, N. Oxford, S.W. Northampton. 5. Most of Oxford. 6. N. Surrey, N.W. Kent. 7. Most of Kent, E. Sussex. 8. W. Somerset, N.E. Devon. 9. Most of Devon, E. Cornwall. 10. W. Cornwall.

CHAPTER XII

A FEW SPECIMENS

THERE is a great wealth of modern dialect literature, as indicated by the lists in the *E.D.D.* Some of these dialect books are poor and inaccurate, and they are frequently spelt according to no intelligible phonetic principles. Yet it not unfrequently happens, as in the works of Sir Walter Scott and Charles Dickens, that the dialectal scraps indicate the pronunciation with tolerable fidelity, which is more than can be said of such portions of their works as are given in the normal spelling. It is curious to notice that writers in dialect are usually, from a phonetic point of view, more careful and consistent in their modes of indicating sounds than are the rest of us. Sometimes their spelling is, accordingly, very good. Those who are interested in this subject may follow up this hint with advantage.

It is impossible to mention even a tithe of the names of our better dialect writers. In Scotland alone there is a large number, some of the more recent bearing such well-known names as those of R. L. Stevenson, George Macdonald (Aberdeen), J. M. Barrie (Forfarshire), and S. R. Crockett (Galloway). Dean Ramsay's humorous *Reminiscences of Scottish Life and Character* must not be passed over. For Ireland we have William Carleton's *Traits and Stories of the Irish Peasantry*, and the novels by Lever and Lover. Cumberland has its delightful stories of *Joe and the Geologist*, and *Bobby Banks' Bodderment*. Cornwall has its *Tales*, by J. T. Tregellas. Devon can boast of R. D. Blackmore, Dorset of Hardy and Barnes, and Lincoln of Tennyson. The literature of Lancashire is vast; it suffices to mention Samuel Bamford, author of *Tummus and Meary*, Ben Brierley, John Byrom, John Collier, author of *Tim Bobbin*, J. P. Morris, author of *T' Lebby Beck Dobby*, and Edwin Waugh, poet. *Giles's Trip to London*, and the other sketches by the same author, are highly characteristic of Norfolk. Northamptonshire has its poet, John Clare; and Suffolk can boast of Robert Bloomfield. According to her own statement, printed in the Preface (p. viii) to the E.D.S. *Bibliographical List*, George Eliot, when writing *Adam Bede*, had in mind "the talk of N. Staffordshire and the neighbouring part of Derbyshire"; whilst, in *Silas Marner*, "the district imagined is in N. Warwickshire." Southey wrote *T' Terrible Knitters e' Dent* in the Westmoreland dialect. Yorkshire, like Lancashire, has a large literature, to which the *E.D.D.* Booklist can alone do justice.

SCOTTISH (Group 3): ABERDEEN.

The following extract is from Chapter XVIII of *Johnny Gibb of Gushetneuk*, by W. Alexander, LL.D., fifteenth edition, Edinburgh, 1908. One special peculiarity of the dialect is the use of *f* for *wh*, as in *fat*, what, *fan*, when. The extract describes how the speaker and his friends went to hear a bellman make a proclamation about the appointment of a new minister to a church.

It's a vera stiff brae, an' ere we wan up to the kirk, it was gyaun upon eleyven o'clock. "Hooever," says the mannie, "we'll be in braw time; it's twal ere the sattlement begin, an' I'se warran they sanna apen the kirk-doors till's till than." So we tak's a luik roun' for ony kent fowk. They war stannin' aboot a'gate roun' aboot the kirk, in scores an' hunners, fowk fae a' the pairis'es roun' aboot, an' some fae hyne awa' as far doon's Marnoch o' the tae han' an' Kintore o' the tither, aw believe; some war stampin' their feet an' slappin' their airms like the yauws o' a win'mill to keep them a-heat; puckles wus sittin' o' the kirk-yard dyke, smokin' an' gyaun on wi' a' kin' o' orra jaw aboot the minaisters, an' aye mair gedderin' in aboot—it was thocht there wus weel on to twa thoosan' there ere a' was deen. An' aye a bit fudder was comin' up fae the manse aboot fat the Presbytery was deein—they war chaumer't there, ye see, wi' the lawvyers an' so on. "Nyod, they maun be sattlin' 'im i' the manse," says ane, "we'll need a' gae doon an' see gin we can win in." "Na, na," says anither, "a bit mair bather aboot thair dissents an' appales bein' ta'en; muckle need they care, wi' sic a Presbytery, fat they try. But here's Johnny Florence, the bellman, at the lang length, I'se be at the boddom o' fat they're at noo." And wi' that he pints till a carlie comin' across the green, wi' a bit paper in's han', an' a gryte squad o' them 't hed been hingin' aboot the manse-door at's tail. "Oo, it's Johnny gyaun to read the edick," cries a gey stoot chap, an' twa three o' them gya a roar o' a lauch...."Speek oot, min!" cries ane. "I think ye mith pronunce some better nor that, Johnny," says anither; an' they interrupit 'im fan he was tryin' to read wi' a' kin' of haivers, takin' the words oot o's mou, an' makin' the uncoest styte o't 't cud be.

NOTES.—*brae*, hill; *wan up*, got up; *gyaun upon*, going close upon; *braw*, excellent; *twal*, twelve; *sattlement*, decision; *I'se*, I will (lit. I shall); *sanna*, will not; *till's*, for us; *kent fowk*, known people, acquaintances; *a'gate*, in all ways; *hunners*, hundreds; *fae*, from; *hyne awa'*, hence away, as far off; *the tae*, the one; *the tither*, the other; *yauws*, sails; *puckles*, numbers, many; *dyke*, stone fence; *orra jaw*, various loud talk; *mair gedderin'*, more gathering; *on to*, near; *deen*, done; *bit fudder*, bit of a rumour (lit. gust of wind); *fae*, from; *fat*, what; *deein*, doing; *chaumer't*, chambered, shut up; *nyod*, a disguised oath; *we'll need*, we must; *gin*, if; *win in*, get in: *bather*, bother; *at the lang length*, at last; *carlie*, churl; *gryte squad*, great crowd; *gey stoot*, rather stout; *twa three*, two or three; *gya*, gave; *mith*, might; *nor that*, than that; *haivers*, foolish talk; *mou*, mouth; *uncoest*, most uncouth, strangest; *styte*, nonsense.

SCOTTISH (Group 7): AYRSHIRE.

The following lines are quoted from a well-known poem by Robert Burns (1759—1796).

THE TWA DOGS (CÆSAR AND LUATH).

Cæs. "I've notic'd, on our Laird's court-day,
An' mony a time my heart's been wae,

Poor tenant bodies, scant o' cash,
How they maun thole a factor's snash:
He'll stamp an' threaten, curse an' swear,
He'll apprehend them, poind their gear;
While they maun stan', wi' aspect humble,
An' hear it a', an' fear and tremble!
I see how folk live that hae riches;
But surely poor folk maun be wretches."

Lu. "They're no sae wretched's ane wad think;
Tho' constantly on poortith's brink,
They're sae accustom'd wi' the sight,
The view o't gies them little fright....
The dearest comfort o' their lives,
Their grushie weans an' faithfu' wives:
The prattling things are just their pride,
That sweetens a' their fire-side....
That merry day the year begins,
They bar the door on frosty win's;
The nappy reeks wi' mantling ream,
An' sheds a heart-inspiring steam;
The luntin' pipe an' sneeshin-mill
Are handed round wi' right good will;
The cantie auld folks crackin' crouse,
The young anes ranting thro' the house—
My heart has been sae fain to see them
That I, for joy, hae barkit wi' them!"...
By this, the sun was out o' sight,
An' darker gloamin' brought the night:
The bum-clock humm'd wi' lazy drone,
The kye stood rowtin' i' the loan;
When up they gat, an' shook their lugs,
Rejoic'd they were na *men* but *dogs*;
An' each took aff his several way,
Resolv'd to meet some ither day.

NOTES.—*wae*, sorrowful; *maun thole*, must endure, must put up with; *factor's snash*, agent's abuse; *poind*, seize upon, sequester; *gear*, property; *hae*, have; *no sae*, not so; *wad*, would; *poortith*, poverty; *grushie*, of thriving growth, well-grown; *weans*, children; *win's*, winds; *nappy*, foaming ale; *reeks*, smokes; *ream*, cream; *luntin'*, smoking, emitting smoke; *sneeshin-mill*, snuff-box; *cantie*, merry; *crackin'*, conversing; *crouse*, with good spirits; *ranting*, running noisily; *fain*, glad; *gloamin'*, twilight; *bum-clock*, beetle (that booms); *kye*, cows; *rowtin'*, lowing; *loan*, milking-place; *lugs*, ears.

SCOTTISH (Group 8): EDINBURGH.

The following stanzas are from *The Farmer's Ingle*, a poem by Robert Fergusson (1750—1774), a native of Edinburgh.

Whan gloming grey out o'er the welkin keeks,
  Whan Batie ca's his owsen to the byre,
Whan Thrasher John, sair dung, his barn-door steeks,
  And lusty lasses at the dighting tire:
What bangs fu' leal the e'enings coming cauld,
  And gars snaw-tappit winter freeze in vain,
Gars dowie mortals look baith blythe and bauld,
  Nor fley'd wi' a' the poortith o' the plain;
  Begin, my Muse, and chant in hamely strain.

Frae the big stack, weel-winnow't on the hill,
  Wi' divets theekit frae the weet and drift,
Sods, peats, and heath'ry trufs the chimley fill,
  And gar their thick'ning smeek salute the lift;
The gudeman, new come hame, is blythe to find,
  Whan he out o'er the halland flings his een,
That ilka turn is handled to his mind,
  That a' his housie looks sae cosh and clean;
  For cleanly house lo'es he, tho' e'er sae mean.

Weel kens the gudewife that the pleughs require
  A heartsome meltith, and refreshing synd
O' nappy liquor, o'er a bleezing fire;
  Sair wark and poortith downa weel be join'd.
Wi' buttered bannocks now the girdle reeks;
  I' the far nook the bowie briskly reams;
The readied kail stands by the chimley-cheeks,
  And hauds the riggin het wi' welcome streams;
  Whilk than the daintiest kitchen nicer seems...

Then a' the house for sleep begin to grien,
  Their joints to slack frae industry a while;
The leaden god fa's heavy on their een,
  And hafflins steeks them frae their daily toil;
The cruizy too can only blink and bleer,
  The restit ingle's done the maist it dow;
Tackman and cottar eke to bed maun steer,
  Upo' the cod to clear their drumly pow,
  Till waukened by the dawning's ruddy glow.

NOTES.—*Ingle*, chimney-corner. *Gloming*, twilight; *keeks*, peeps; *ca's*, drives (lit. calls); *owsen*, oxen; *byre*, cow-house; *sair dung*, sorely tired; *steeks*, shuts; *dighting*, winnowing; *bangs fu' leal*, defeats right well; *gars*, makes; *-tappit*, crested; *dowie*, melancholy; *fley'd*, frighted; *poortith*, poverty.

Divets, turfs; *theekit*, thatched; *weet*, wet; *sods, peats, and heath'ry trufs*, various turf fuels; *chimley*, fire-place; *gar*, make; *smeek*, smoke; *lift*, sky; *halland*, partition forming a screen; *een*, eyes; *ilka*, each; *cosh*, cosy; *lo'es*, loves.

Kens, knows; *meltith*, meal-tide, meal; *synd*, wash-down, draught; *nappy*, heady, strong; *downa*, cannot; *bannocks*, cakes; *girdle*, hot-plate; *reeks*, smokes; *bowie*, cask, beer-barrel; *reams*, foams; *readied kail*, (dish of) cooked greens; *by*, beside; *hauds...het*, keeps...hot; *riggin*, roof over the open hearth; *whilk*, which.

Grien, yearn, long; *hafflins steeks*, half shuts; *cruizy*, oil-lamp; *bleer*, bedim (the sight); *restit ingle*, made up fire; *dow*, can; *tackman*, lease-holder, farmer; *cod*, pillow; *drumly pow*, confused head.

NORTHERN (ENGLAND); Group 2: WESTMORELAND.

The following extract is from a remarkable tract entitled *A Bran New Wark, by William De Worfat*; Kendal, 1785. The author was the Rev. William Hutton, Rector of Beetham in Westmoreland, 1762—1811, and head of a family seated at Overthwaite (here called Worfat) in that parish. It was edited by me for the E.D.S. in 1879.

Last Saturday sennet, abaut seun in the evening (twas lownd and fraaze hard) the stars twinkled, and the setting moon cast gigantic shadows. I was stalking hameward across Blackwater-mosses, and whistling as I tramp'd for want of thought, when a noise struck my ear, like the crumpling of frosty murgeon; it made me stop short, and I thought I saw a strange form before me: it vanished behint a windraw; and again thare was nought in view but dreary dykes, and dusky ling. An awful silence reigned araund; this was sean brokken by a skirling hullet; sure nivver did hullet, herrensue, or miredrum, mak sic a noise before. Your minister [*himself*] was freetned, the hairs of his head stood an end, his blead storkened, and the haggard creature moving slawly nearer, the mirkiness of the neet shew'd her as big again as she was...She stoup'd and drop'd a poak, and thus began with a whining tone. "Deary me! deary me! forgive me, good Sir, but this yance, I'll steal naa maar. This seck is elding to keep us fra starving!"...[*The author visits the poor woman's cottage.*] She sat on a three-legg'd steal, and a dim coal smook'd within the rim of a brandreth, oor which a seety rattencreak hung dangling fra a black randletree. The walls were plaister'd with dirt, and a stee, with hardly a rung, was rear'd into a loft. Araund the woman her lile ans sprawl'd on the hearth, some whiting speals, some snottering and crying, and ya ruddy-cheek'd lad threw on a bullen to make a loww, for its mother to find her loup. By this sweal I beheld this family's poverty.

NOTES.—*Sennet*, seven nights, week; *seun*, seven; *lownd*, still, calm; *murgeon*, rubbish earth cut up and thrown aside in order to get peat; *windraw*, heap of dug earth; *ling*, kind of heather; *skirling hullet*, shrieking owlet; *herrensue*, young heron; *miredrum*, bittern; *blead storkened*, blood congealed; *neet*, night; *poak*, bag; *yance*, once; *seck*, sack, i.e. contents of this sack; *elding*, fuel; *steal*, stool; *brandreth*, iron frame over the fire; *seaty*, sooty; *rattencreak*, pot-crook, pothook; *randletree*, a beam from which the pothook hangs; *stee*, ladder; *loft*, upper room; *lile ans*, little ones; *whiting speals*, whittling small sticks; *snottering*, sobbing; *ya*, one; *bullen*, hemp-stalk; *loww*, flame; *loup*, loop, stitch in knitting; *sweal*, blaze.

MIDLAND (Group 1): LINCOLN.

I here give a few quotations from the Glossary of Words used in the Wapentakes of Manley and Corringham, Lincolnshire, by E. Peacock, F.S.A.; 2nd ed., E.D.S., 1889. The illustrative sentences are very characteristic.

Beal, to bellow.—Th' bairn beäled oot that bad, I was clëan scar'd, but it was at noht bud a battle-twig 'at hed crohled up'n his airm. (*Battle-twig*, earwig; *airm*, arm.)

Cart, to get into, to get into a bad temper.—Na, noo, thoo neädn't get into th' cart, for I weän't draw thee.

Cauf, a calf, silly fellow.—A gentleman was enlarging to a Winterton lad on the virtues of Spanish juice [liquorice water]. "Ah, then, ye'll ha' been to th' mines, wheäre thaay gets it," the boy exclaimed; whereupon the mother broke in with—"A greät cauf! Duz he think 'at thaay dig it oot o' th' grund, saäme as thaay do sugar?"

Chess, a tier.—I've been tell'd that e' plaaces wheäre thaay graw silk-worms, thaay keäps 'em on traays, chess aboon chess, like cheney i' a cupboard. (*E'*, in ; *cheney*, china.)

Clammer, to climb.—Oor Uriah's clammered into th' parson's cherry-tree, muther, an' he is swalla'in on 'em aboon a bit. I shouldn't ha tell'd ye nobbut he weänt chuck me ony doon. (*Nobbut*, only.)

Cottoner, something very striking.—Th' bairn hed been e' mischief all daay thrif; at last, when I was sidin' awaay th' teä-things, what duz he do but tum'le i'to th' well. So, says I, Well, this is a cottoner; we shall hev to send for Mr Iveson (the coroner) noo, I reckon. (*Thrif*, through ; *sidin' awaay*, putting away.)

Ducks.—A girl said to the author, of a woman with whom she had been living for a short time as servant, "I'd raather be nibbled to deäd wi' ducks then live with Miss P. She's alus a natterin'." (*Deäd*, death ; *alus*, always ; *natterin'*, nagging.)

Good mind, strong intention.—She said she'd a good mind to hing her-sen, soä I ax'd if I mud send for Mr Holgate (the coroner), to be ready like. (*Hing*, hang ; *mud*, might.)

Jaup, senseless talk.—Ho'd the jaup wi' thĕ ; dos't ta want ivery body to knaw how soft thoo is? (*Ho'd*, hold ; *soft*, foolish.)

MIDLAND (Group 2): S.E. LANCASHIRE.

The following poem is from *Poems and Songs* by Edwin Waugh ; 3rd ed., London, 1870.

OWD PINDER.

Owd Pinder were a rackless foo,
An' spent his days i' spreein' ;
At th' end ov every drinkin-do,
He're sure to crack o' deein' ;
"Go, sell my rags, an' sell my shoon,
Aw's never live to trail 'em ;
My ballis-pipes are eawt o' tune,
An' th' wynt begins to fail 'em !

Eawr Matty's very fresh an' yung;—
  'T would any mon bewilder;—
Hoo'll wed again afore it's lung,
  For th' lass is fond o' childer;
My bit o' brass 'll fly—yo'n see—
  When th' coffin-lid has screen'd me—
It gwos again my pluck to dee,
  An' lev her wick beheend me.

Come, Matty, come, an' cool my yed;
  Aw'm finish'd, to my thinkin';"
Hoo happed him nicely up, an' said,
  "Thae'st brought it on wi' drinkin'."—
"Nay, nay," said he, "my fuddle's done,
  We're partin' tone fro tother;
So promise me that, when aw'm gwon,
  Thea'll never wed another!"

"Th' owd tale," said hoo, an' laft her stoo;
  "It's rayly past believin';
Thee think o' th' world thea'rt goin' to,
  An' lev this world to th' livin';
What use to me can deeod folk be?
  Thae's kilt thisel' wi' spreein';
An' iv that's o' thae wants wi' me,
  Get forrud wi' thi deein'!"

NOTES.—*Owd*, old; *rackless foo*, reckless fool; *spreein'*, merry-making, drinking; *-do*, bout; *He're*, he would be; *crack o' deein'*, hint at dying; *Aw's*, I shall; *trail*, walk in; *ballis-pipes*, bellows-pipes, lungs; *eawt*, out; *wynt*, wind.

Eawr, our, my; *Hoo*, she; *brass*, money; *yo'n*, you will; *lev*, leave; *wick*, quick, i.e. alive.

Yed, head; *happed*, covered; *fuddle*, drinking-bout; *tone fro tother*, the one from the other.

Stoo, stool; *Thee think*, do thou think; *deeod*, dead; *o'*, all; *get forrud*, get on, go on.

MIDLAND (Group 5): SHEFFIELD.

The following extract is from A. Bywater's *Sheffield Dialect*, 3rd ed., 1877; as quoted in S. O. Addy's *Sheffield Glossary*, E.D.S., 1888, p. xv.

Jerra Flatback. Hah, they'n better toimes on't nah, booath e heitin and clooas; we'n had menni a mess a nettle porridge an brawis on a Sunda mo'nin, for us brekfast...Samma, dusta remember hah menni names we had for sahwer wotcake?

Oud Samma Squarejoint. O kno'n't, lad; bur o think we'd foive or six. Let's see: Slammak wer won, an' Flat-dick wer anuther; an't tuther wor—a dear, mo memra fails ma—Flannel an' Jonta; an-an-an-an—bless me, wot a thing it is tubbe oud, mo memra gers war for ware, bur o kno heah's anuther; o'st think on enah.—A, Jerra, heah's menni a thahsand dogs nah days, at's better dun too nor we wor then; an them were t'golden days a Hallamshoir, they sen. An they happen wor, for't mesters. Hofe at prentis lads e them days wor lether'd whoile ther skin wor skoi-blue, and clam'd whoile ther booans wer bare, an work'd whoile they wor as knock-kneed as oud Nobbletistocks. Thah nivver sees nooa knock-kneed cutlers nah: nou, not sooa; they'n better mesters nah, an they'n better sooat a wark anole. They dooant mezher em we a stick, as oud Natta Hall did. But for all that, we'd none a yer wirligig polishin; nor Tom Dockin scales, wit bousters comin off; nor yer sham stag, nor sham revvits, an sich loik. T' noives wor better made then, Jerra.

Jerra: Hah, they wor better made; they made t' noives for yuse then, but they mayn em to sell nah.

NOTES.—Observe *'n* for *han* (plural), have; *on't nah*, of it now; *e heitin*, in eating; *mess a*, dish of, meal of; *brawis*, brose, porridge; *hah*, how; *sahwer wotcake*, leavened oatcake; *bur o*, but I; *mo*, my; *ma*, me; *tubbe oud*, to be old; *gers*, gets; *war for ware*, worse for wear; *o'st*, I shall; *think on*, remember; *enah*, presently; *nah days*, nowadays; *at's*, that are; *dun too*, treated; *nor we*, than we; *Hallamshoir*, Hallamshire, the district including Sheffield and the neighbourhood; *sen*, say; *happen*, perhaps; *for't*, for the; *hofe at*, half of the; *e them*, in those; *lether'd*, beaten; *whoile*, till; *clam'd* (for *clamm'd*), starved; *sooat a*, sort of; *anole*, and all; *we*, with; *wirligig*, machine; *Tom Dockin scales*, scales cut out of thin rolled iron instead of being forged; *bousters*, bolsters (a *bolster* is a lump of metal between the tang and the blade of a knife); *stag*, stag-horn handle (?); *mayn*, pl. make.

Midland (Group 6): Cheshire.

The following extract is from "Betty Bresskittle's Pattens, or Sanshum Fair," by J. C. Clough; printed with Holland's *Cheshire Glossary*, E.D.S. (1886), p. 466. Sanshum or Sanjem Fair is a fair held at Altrincham on St James's Day.

Jud sprung upo' th' stage leet as a buck an' bowd as a dandy-cock, an' th' mon what were playingk th' drum (only it wer'nt a gradely drum) gen him a pair o' gloves. Jud began a-sparringk, an' th' foaks shaouted, "Hooray! Go it, owd Jud! Tha'rt a gradely Cheshire mon!"

Th' black felly next gen Jud a wee bit o' a bang i' th' reet ee, an Jud git as weild as weild, an hit reet aht, but some hah he couldna git a gradely bang at th' black mon. At-aftur two or three minutes th' black felly knocked Jud dahn, an t'other chap coom and picked him up, an' touch'd Jud's faace wi' th' spunge everywheer wheer he'd getten a bang, but th' spunge had getten a gurt lot o' red ruddle on it, so that it made gurt red blotches upo' Jud's faace wheer it touched it; an th' foaks shaouted and shaouted, "Hooray, Jud! Owd mon! at em agen!" An Jud let floy a good un, an th' mon wi' th' spunge had to pick th' blackeymoor up this toime an put th' ruddle upo' his faace just at-under th'ee.

"Hooray, Jud! hooray, owd mon!" shaouted Jock Carter o' Runjer; "tha'rt game, if tha'rt owd!"

Just at that vary minit Jud's weife, bad as hoo were wi' th' rheumatic, pushed her rooäd through th' foaks, and stood i' th' frunt o' th' show.

"Go it agen, Jud! here's th' weife coom t'see hah gam tha art!" shaouted Jonas.

Jud turn'd rahnd an gurned at th' frunt o' th' show wi' his faace aw ruddle.

"Tha girt soo! I'll baste thi when aw get thi hwom, that aw will!" shaouted Betty Bresskittle; "aw wunder tha artna ashamed o' thisen, to stond theer a-feightingk th' deevil hissel!"

Notes.—*Jud*, for George; *leet*, light; *bowd*, bold; *dandycock*, Bantam cock; *gradely*, proper; *gen*, gave; *owd*, old; *reet ee*, right eye; *git*, got; *as weild as weild*, as wild as could be; *aht*, out; *at-aftur*, after; *gurt*, great; *em*, him; *floy*, fly; *Runjer*, Ringway; *game* (also *gam*), full of pluck; *hoo*, she; *rooad*, road, way; *gurned*, grinned; *soo*, sow (term of abuse); *hwom*, home; *thisen*, thyself.

Eastern (Group 2): N. Essex.

The following extract is from *John Noakes and Mary Styles*, by Charles Clark, of Great Totham; London, 1839. Reprinted for the E.D.S., 1895. As Great Totham is to the North of Maldon, I take this specimen to belong to Prof. Wright's "Division 2" rather than to the S.W. Essex of "Division 5." The use of *w* for initial *v* occurs frequently, as in *werry*, very, etc.

At Tottum's Cock-a-Bevis Hill,
  A sput surpass'd by few,
Where toddlers ollis haut to eye
  The proper pritty wiew,

Where people crake so ov the place,
  Leas-ways, so I've hard say;
An' frum its top yow, sarteny,
  Can see a monsus way.

But no sense ov a place, some think,
  Is this here hill so high,—
'Cos there, full oft, 'tis nation coad,
  But that don't argufy.

As sum'dy, 'haps, when nigh the sput,
  May ha' a wish to see 't,—
From Mauldon toun to Keldon 'tis,
  An' 'gin a four-releet.

At Cock-a-Bevis Hill, too, the
  Wiseacres show a tree
Which if you clamber up, besure,
  A precious way yow see.

I dorn't think I cud clime it now,
  Aldoe I uster cud;
I shudn't warsley loike to troy,
  For gulch cum down I shud.

My head 'ood swim,—I 'oodn't do't
  Nut even fur a guinea;
A naarbour ax'd me, t'other day;
  "Naa, naa," says I, "nut quinny."

Notes.—*Sput*, spot; *toddlers*, walkers; *ollis*, always; *haut*, halt; *wiew*, view.

Crake, boast; *leas(t)ways*, at least; *sarteny*, certainly; *monsus*, monstrous, very long.

No sense ov a, poor, bad; *coad*, cold; *argufy*, prove (anything).

Sum'dy, somebody; *from M.*, between Maldon and Kelvedon; *'gin*, against, near; *four-releet* (originally *four-e leet*, lit. "ways of four," *four-e* being the genitive plural, hence) meeting of four roads.

Dorn't, don't; *aldoe*, although; *uster cud* (for *us'd to could*), used to be able; *warsley*, vastly, much; *loike*, like; *gulch*, heavily, with a bang.

'Ood, would; *nut*, not; *ax'd*, asked; *naa*, no; *nut quinny*, not quite, not at all.

EASTERN (Group 3): NORFOLK.

The following extract from "A Norfolk Dialogue" is from a work entitled *Erratics by a Sailor*, printed anonymously at London in 1800, and written by the Rev. Joshua Larwood, rector of Swanton Morley, near East Dereham. Most of the words are quite familiar to me, as I was curate of East Dereham in 1861–2, and heard the dialect daily. The whole dialogue was reprinted in *Nine Specimens of English Dialects*; E.D.S., 1895.

The Dialogue was accompanied by "a translation," as here reprinted. It renders a glossary needless.

ORIGINAL VULGAR NORFOLK.	TRANSLATION.
Narbor Rabbin and Narbor Tibby.	*Neighbour Robin and Neighbour Stephen.*
R. Tibby, d'ye know how the knacker's mawther Nutty du?	*R.* Stephen, do you know how the collar-maker's daughter Ursula is?
T. Why, i' facks, Rabbin,	*S.* Why, in fact, Robin, she

she's nation cothy; by Goms, she is so snasty that I think she is will-led.

is extremely sick; by (*obsolete*), she is so snarlish, that I think she's out of her mind.

R. She's a fate mawther, but ollas in dibles wi' the knacker and thackster; she is ollas a-ating o' thapes and dodmans. The fogger sa, she ha the black sap; but the grosher sa, she have an ill dent.

R. She's a clever girl, but always in troubles with the collar-maker and thatcher; she is always eating gooseberries and snails. The man at the chandler's shop says she has a consumption: but the grocer says she's out of her senses.

T. Why, ah! tother da she fared stounded: she pluck'd the pur from the back-stock, and copped it agin the balk of the douw-pollar, and barnt it; and then she hulled [it] at the thackster, and hart his weeson, and huckle-bone. There was northing but cadders in the douw-pollar, and no douws: and so, arter she had barnt the balk, and the door-stall, and the plancher, she run into the par-yard, thru the pytle, and then swounded behinn'd a sight o' gotches o' beergood.

S. Why, aye! the other day she appeared struck mad: she snatched the poker from the back of the stove, and flung it against the beam of the pigeon-house, and burnt it; and then she throwed it at the thatcher, and hurt his throat and hip-bone. There were no pigeons in the pigeon-house, and nothing but jack-daws; and so, after she had burned the beam, and the door-frame and the floor, she ran into the cow-yard, through the small field, and fainted behind several pitchers of yeast.

R. Ah, the shummaker told me o' that rum rig; and his nevvey sa, that the beer-good was fystey; and that Nutty was so swelter'd, that she ha got a pain in spade-bones. The

R. Aye, the shoemaker told me of that comical trick; and his nephew says, that the yeast was musty; and that Ursula [was so] smothered, that she has got a pain in her blade-

thacker wou'd ha gin har some doctor's gear in a beaker; but he sa she'll niver moize agin.	bones. The thatcher would have given her some doctor's medicine in a tumbler; but he says, she will never recover.

NOTES.—Pronounce *du* like E. *dew*. *Snasty*, pron. *snaisty*, cross. *Fate*, *fait* (cf. E. *feat*), suitable, clever. *Mawther*, a young girl; Norw. *moder*. *Dibles*: the *i* is long. *Sa*, says; *ha*, *have*, has; note the absence of final *s* in the third person singular. *Cadder*, for *caddow*; from *caa-daw*, cawing daw. *Douw*, for *dow*, a dove. *Par*: for *parrock*, a paddock. *Fystey*: with long *y*, from *foist*, a fusty smell. *Sweltered*, over-heated, in profuse perspiration. *Moize*, thrive, mend.

WESTERN (Group 1): S.W. SHROPSHIRE.

The following specimen is given in Miss Jackson's *Shropshire Word-book*, London, 1879, p. xciv. It describes how Betty Andrews, of Pulverbatch, rescued her little son, who had fallen into the brook.

I 'eärd a scrike, ma'am, an' I run, an' theer I sid Frank 'ad pecked i' the bruck an' douked under an' wuz drowndin', an' I jumped after 'im an' got 'out on 'im an' lugged 'im on to the bonk all sludge, an' I got 'im wham afore our Sam comen in—a good job it wuz for Sam as 'e wunna theer an' as Frank wunna drownded, for if 'e 'ad bin I should 'a' tore our Sam all to winder-rags, an' then 'e 'd a bin djed an' Frank drownded an' I should a bin 'anged. I toud Sam wen 'e tŏŏk the 'ouse as I didna like it.—"Bless the wench," 'e sed, "what'n'ee want? Theer's a tidy 'ouse an' a good garden an' a run for the pig." "Aye," I sed, "an' a good bruck for the childern to peck in;" so if Frank 'ad bin drownded I should a bin the djeth uv our Sam. I wuz that frittened, ma'am, that I didna spake for a nour after I got wham, an' Sam sed as 'e 'adna sid me quiet so lung sence we wun married, an' that wuz eighteen 'ear.

NOTES.—Miss Jackson adds the pronunciation, in glossic notation. There is no sound of initial *h*. *Scrike*, shriek; *sid*, seed, i.e. saw; *pecked*, pitched, fallen headlong; *bruck*, brook; *douked*, ducked; *'out*, hold; *bonk*, bank; *wham*, home; *wunna*, was not; *winder-rags*, shreds; *djed*, dead; *toud*, told; *what'n'ee*, what do you; *a nour*, an hour; *sid*, seen; *lung*, long; *wun*, were.

SOUTHERN (Group 2): WILTSHIRE.

The following well-known Wiltshire fable is from *Wiltshire Tales*, by J. Yonge Akerman (1853). I give it as it stands in the Preface to Halliwell's Dictionary; omitting the "Moral."

THE HARNET AND THE BITTLE.

A harnet zet in a hollur tree—
A proper spiteful twoad was he;
And a merrily zung while he did zet
His stinge as shearp as a bagganet;
  Oh, who so vine and bowld as I?
  I vears not bee, nor wapse, nor vly!

A bittle up thuck tree did clim,
And scarnvully did look at him;
Zays he, "Zur harnet, who giv thee
A right to zet in thuck there tree?
  Vor ael you zengs so nation vine,
  I tell 'e 'tis a house o' mine!"

The harnet's conscience velt a twinge,
But grawin' bowld wi' his long stinge,
Zays he, "Possession's the best laaw;
Zo here th' sha'sn't put a claaw!
  Be off, and leave the tree to me,
  The mixen's good enough for thee!"

Just then a yuckel, passin' by,
Was axed by them the cause to try;
"Ha! ha! I zee how 'tis!" zays he,
"They'll make a vamous munch vor me!"
His bill was shearp, his stomach lear,
Zo up a snapped the caddlin' pair!

NOTES.—Observe *z* and *v* for initial *s* and *f*; *harnet*, hornet; *bittle*, beetle; *zet*, sat; *proper*, very; *twoad*, toad, wretch; *a*, he; *stinge*, sting; *bagganet*, bayonet.

Thuck, that; *clim*, climb; *giv*, gave; *zet*, sit; *ael*, all.

Th' sha'sn't, thou shalt not; *mixen*, dung-heap.

Yuckel, woodpecker; *axed*, asked; *vamous munch*, excellent meal; *lear*, empty; *caddlin'*, quarrelsome.

SOUTHERN (Group 3): ISLE OF WIGHT.

The following colloquy is quoted in the *Glossary of Isle of Wight Words*, E.D.S., 1881, at p. 50.

I recollect perfectly the late Mr James Phillips of Merston relating a dialogue that occurred between two of his labourers relative to the word *straddle-bob*, a beetle....At the time of luncheon, one of them, on taking his *bren-cheese* (bread and cheese) out of a little bag, saw something that had found its way there; which led to the following discourse.

Jan. What's got there, you?

Will. A straddlebob craalun about in the nammut-bag.

J. Straddlebob? Where dedst leyarn to caal 'n by that neyam?

W. Why, what shoud e caal 'n? 'Tes the right neyam, esn ut?

J. Right neyam? No! Why, ye gurt zote vool, casn't zee 'tes a dumbledore?

W. I know 'tes; but vur aal that, straddlebob's zo right a neyam vor 'n as dumbledore ez.

J. Come, I'll be blamed if I doant laay thee a quart o' that.

W. Done! and I'll ax Meyastur to-night when I goos whoam, bee't how't wool.

Accordingly, Meyastur was applied to by Will, who made his decision known to Jan the next morning.

W. I zay, Jan! I axed Meyastur about that are last night.

J. Well, what ded ur zay?

W. Why, a zed one neyam ez jest zo vittun vor'n as tother; and he lowz a ben caal'd straddlebob ever zunce the Island was vust meyad.

J. Well, if that's the keeas, I spooas I lost the quart.

W. That thee hast, lucky; and we'll goo down to Arreton to the Rid Lion and drink un ater we done work.

NOTES.—Observe *z* for *s*, and *v* for *f* initially. *What's*, What hast thou; *nammut* (lit. noon-meat), luncheon, usually eaten at 9 A.M. (*nōna hōra*); *leyarn*, learn; *esn*, is not; *gurt*, great; *zote*, soft, silly; *casn't*, canst not; *laay*, lay, wager; *how't wool*, how it will; *that are*, that there; *lowz* (lit. allows), opines; *zunce*, since; *vust meyad*, first made; *keeas*, case; *lucky*, look ye!

SOUTHERN (Group 7): EAST SUSSEX.

The following quotations are from the *Dictionary of the Sussex Dialect*, by the Rev. W. D. Parish, Vicar of Selmeston; E.D.S. 1875. The Glossary refers rather to E. than to W. Sussex, Selmeston being between Lewes and Eastbourne.

Call over, to abuse. "He come along here a-cadging, and fancy he just did call me over, because I told him as I hadn't got naun to give him." (*Naun*, nothing.)

Clocksmith, a watchmaker. "I be quite lost about time, I be; for I've been forced to send my watch to the clocksmith. I couldn't make no sense of mending it myself; for I'd iled it and I'd biled it, and then I couldn't do more with it."

Cocker-up, to spoil; to gloss over with an air of truth. "You see this here chap of hers, he's cockered-up some story about having to goo away somewheres up into the sheeres; and I tell her she's no call to be so cluck over it; and for my part I dunno but what I be very glad an't, for he was a chap as was always a-cokeing about the cupboards, and cogging her out of a Sunday." (*The sheeres*, any shire of England except Kent and Sussex; *call*, reason; *cluck*, out of spirits; *coke*, to peep; *cog*, to entice.)

Joy, a jay. "Poor old Master Crockham, he's in terrible order, surelý! The meece have taken his peas, and the joys have got at his beans, and the snags have spilt all his lettuce." (*Order*, bad temper; *meece*, mice; *snags*, snails; *spilt*, spoilt.)

Kiddle, to tickle. "Those thunder-bugs did kiddle me so that I couldn't keep still no hows." (*Thunder-bug*, a midge.)

Lawyer, a long bramble full of thorns, so called because, "when once they gets a holt an ye, ye doänt easy get shut of 'em."

Leetle, a diminutive of little. "I never see one of these here gurt men there's s'much talk about in the peapers, only once, and that was up at Smiffle Show adunnamany years agoo. Prime minister, they told me he was, up at London; a leetle, lear, miserable, skinny-looking chap as ever I see. 'Why,' I says, 'we doänt count our minister to be much, but he's a deal primer-looking than what yourn be.'" (*Gurt*, great; *Smiffle*, Smithfield; *adunnamany*, I don't know how many; *lear*, thin, hungry; *see*, saw.)

Sarment, a sermon. "I likes a good long sarment, I doos; so as when you wakes up it ain't all over."

Tempory (temporary), slight, badly finished. "Who be I? Why, I be John Carbury, that's who I be! And who be you? Why, you ain't a man at all, you ain't! You be naun but a poor tempory creetur run up by contract, that's what you be!"

Tot, a bush; a tuft of grass. "There warn't any grass at all when we fust come here; naun but a passel o' gurt old tots and tussicks. You see there was one of these here new-fashioned men had had the farm, and he'd properly starved the land and the labourers, and the cattle and everything, without it was hisself." (*Passel*, parcel; *tussicks*, tufts of rank grass.)

Twort (for *thwart*), pert and saucy. "She's terrible twort—she wants a good setting down, she do; and she'll get it too. Wait till my master comes in!"

Winterpicks, blackthorn berries.

Winter-proud, cold. "When you sees so many of these here winterpicks about, you may be pretty sure 'twill be middlin' winter-proud."

BIBLIOGRAPHY

Ancren Riwle; ed. Jas. Morton. Camden Soc., 1873. (About 1230.)

Anglo-Saxon and Early English Psalter. Surtees Society. London, 1843–7. 2 vols. (See p. 25.)

Beda.—Venerabilis Bedae Historiae Ecclesiasticae Gentis Anglorum Libri III, IV; ed. J. E. B. Mayor, M.A. and J. R. Lumby, B.D. Cambridge, 1878.

—— The Venerable Bede's Ecclesiastical History; also the Anglo-Saxon Chronicle (both in English). Ed. J. A. Giles, D.C.L. London, 1859. (In Bohn's Library.)

Dictionaries containing dialect words. (See p. 100.)

Durham Ritual.—Rituale Ecclesiæ Dunelmensis. Surtees Society. London, 1840.

Earle, Rev. J.; Anglo-Saxon Literature. London, S.P.C.K., 1884.

E.D.D.—English Dialect Dictionary (to which is appended the English Dialect Grammar); ed. Dr Joseph Wright. Oxford, 1898—1905.

E.D.S.—English Dialect Society, publications of the. London, 1873–96.

E.E.T.S.—Early English Text Society, publications of the. London, 1864—1910. (Contains Alliterative Poems, Ayenbite of Inwyt, Barbour's Bruce, Sir Gawayne and the Grene Knight St Juliana, Kentish Sermons, Lyndesay's Works, etc.)

Jackson, Miss.—Shropshire Wordbook, by Georgina F. Jackson. London, 1879.

Jamieson's Scottish Dictionary. A new edition, ed. J. Longmuir and D. Donaldson. Paisley, 1879–87. 4to. 4 vols. and Supplement.

Layamon's Brut; ed. Sir F. Madden. London, 1847. 3 vols.

Minot's Poems; ed. J. Hall. Oxford, 1887.

Morris, Rev. R., LL.D.; The Blickling Homilies. (E.E.T.S.) London, 1880.

—— Old English Miscellany. (E.E.T.S.) London, 1872.

—— Old English Homilies, Series I and II. (E.E.T.S.) London, 1867 and 1873.

—— Specimens of Early English. Part I. 1150—1300. Second Edition. Oxford, 1885.

Morris, Rev. R. and Skeat, Rev. W. W.; Specimens of Early English. Part II. Third edition. Oxford, 1894.

Murray, Sir James A. H. The Dialect of the Southern Counties of Scotland. (Phil. Soc.) London, 1873.

N.E.D.—The New English Dictionary; by Sir James A. H. Murray, H. Bradley, and W. A. Craigie. Oxford, 1888—.

Ormulum; ed. R. M. White. Oxford, 1852. 2 vols.

Pricke of Conscience, by Richard Rolle de Hampole; ed. R. Morris. (Phil. Soc.) London, 1863.

Psalter, by R. Rolle de Hampole; ed. Rev. H. R. Bramley. Oxford, 1884.

Robert of Gloucester; ed. W. Aldis Wright. (Record Series.) London, 1887. 2 vols.

Skeat, Rev. Walter W.; The Chaucer Canon. Oxford, 1900.

—— Etymological English Dictionary. New edition. Oxford, 1910.

—— The Holy Gospels, in Anglo-Saxon, Northumbrian, and Mercian Versions. Cambridge, 1871–87.

—— Primer of English Etymology. Fifth edition. Oxford, 1910.

—— Principles of English Etymology, Series I. Second edition. Oxford, 1892.

Sweet, H.; An Anglo-Saxon Reader. Seventh edition. Oxford, 1894.

—— A Second Anglo-Saxon Reader, Archaic and Dialectal. Oxford, 1887.

—— The Oldest English Texts. (E.E.T.S.) London, 1885.

Trevisa.—Higden's Polychronicon; with Trevisa's English Version; ed. C. Babington, B.D., and the Rev. J. R. Lumby, D.D. (Record Series.) 9 vols. London, 1865–86.

Wise, J. R.; Shakspere, his Birthplace and its Neighbourhood. London, 1861.

INDEX

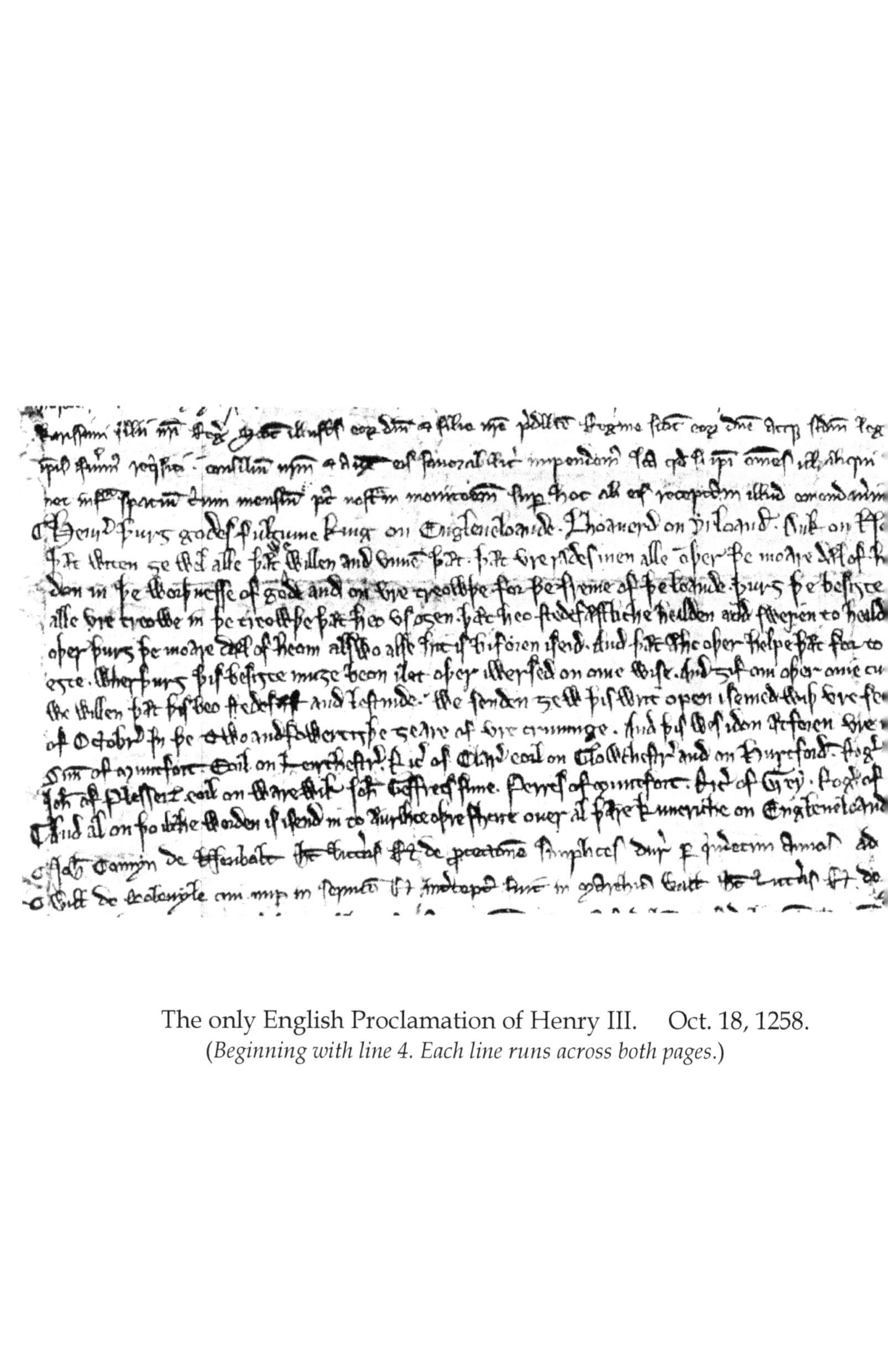

The only English Proclamation of Henry III. Oct. 18, 1258.

(*Beginning with line 4. Each line runs across both pages.*)

[illegible]

tenas consuetudines illi regem chartam Walteri pro Standine in eisdem negotio ... indignerit et ab

aliquis eorum super premissis in aliquo deliquerint et inde requisiti fuerint super emendas gerende faciende

eam ut debuerint in nullo gerunt eas tam volumus. In cuius etc. T. R. apud Westm. xviij die Octobr.

on Aquitain and eorl on Aniow Send igretinge to alle hise halde ilærde and ileawede on Huntendon schir'.

þæt beoþ ichosen þurȝ us and þurȝ þæt loandes folk on vre kuneriche habbeþ idon and schullen

þan to foreniseide redesmen. beo stedefæst and ilestinde in alle þinge abuten ænde. And we hoaten

and to werien þo isetnesses þæt beon makede and beon to makien þurȝ þan to foren iseide redesmen

e bi þan ilche oþe aȝenes alle men. Riȝt for to done and to foangen. And noan ne nime of loande ne of

her onȝenes. we willen and hoaten þæt alle vre treowe heom healden deadliche ifoan. And for þæt

o halden amanges ȝew ine hord. Witnesse vs seluen æt Lunden. þane Eȝtetenþe day. on þe Monþ

nene redesmen. Boneface Archebischop on Kanterbur'. Walt' of Cantelow. Bischop on Wirechestr'.

od eorl on Northfolk and Marescal on Engleneloand'. Perres of Sauueye. Will' of Fort eorl on Aubem'

temer. Iames of Aldithel and ætforen oþre inoȝe.

And ek in tel Irelonde.

mondum Consimilis litere. T. R. apud Westm. xx die Octobr.

[illegible]

www.ingramcontent.com/pod-product-compliance
Ingram Content Group UK Ltd.
Pitfield, Milton Keynes, MK11 3LW, UK
UKHW020129250726
13967UKWH00002B/548